In the Sacred Pause

In the Sacred Pause

Liturgies for times of stillness and waiting

Claire Brockelsby
Ian Henderson
Mary Kilikidi
and
Daniel Krawczyk

CANTERBURY
PRESS

© Claire Brockelsby, Ian Henderson, Mary Kilikidi and Daniel Krawczyk 2025

Published in 2025 by Canterbury Press
Editorial office
3rd Floor, Invicta House,
110 Golden Lane,
London EC1Y 0TG, UK
www.canterburypress.co.uk

Canterbury Press is an imprint of Hymns Ancient & Modern Ltd
(a registered charity)

Ancient
&Modern

Hymns Ancient & Modern® is a registered trademark of
Hymns Ancient & Modern Ltd
13A Hellesdon Park Road, Norwich,
Norfolk NR6 5DR, UK

Scripture quotations are from New Revised Standard Version Bible: Anglicised
Edition, copyright © 1989, 1995 National Council of the Churches of Christ in
the United States of America. Used by permission. All rights reserved worldwide.

ISBN: 978-1-78622-686-0

British Library Cataloguing in Publication data
A catalogue record for this book is available
from the British Library

EU GPSR Authorised Representative
LOGOS EUROPE, 9 rue Nicolas Poussin, 17000, LA ROCHELLE, France
E-mail: Contact@logoseurope.eu

Typeset by Regent Typesetting
Printed and bound by
CPI Group (UK) Ltd

Contents

Authors' Preface

In the Sacred Pause began as an assignment but evolved into something much deeper and more significant: a liturgical offering shaped by the varied experiences and perspectives of its authors. What started as an academic endeavour quickly transformed into a living project that now serves as an aid for ministry, and as a source of comfort for those navigating the complexities of trauma within faith communities.

The authors, Claire Brockelsby, Ian Henderson, Mary Kilikidi and Daniel Krawczyk, came together as ordinands during their theological studies, bringing with them a rich tapestry of cultural backgrounds, experiences and theological traditions. Among them are those who grew up in the Anglican tradition, those who are new to faith and the Anglican Church, and those who have experienced Orthodox, Catholic and Lutheran churches. With roots in places as diverse as Russia and Poland, their perspectives reflect the global nature of the Church and the varied experiences that trauma can encompass. The energy and excitement that arose from the group's first discussion on this topic underscored the importance of their task: to create resources that are trauma-oriented and trauma-informed.

Karen O'Donnell, a renowned trauma theologian and Academic Dean at Westcott House, has contributed the Foreword, positioning these liturgies within the ongoing development of Trauma Theology. It was under the guidance of O'Donnell and other faculty members that this project took shape, inspired by a module that sought to explore how theological reflection through a trauma lens can intersect with pastoral care and public ministry.

The liturgies within this volume are designed with an acute sensitivity to the realities of trauma. While the authors are not trauma experts, their engagement with Trauma Theology through study, ministry practice and personal experiences has informed this resource. These liturgies, shaped by the authors' lived experiences and academic reflection, aim to be adaptable, allowing leaders to use them within their own contexts to foster environments where individuals can encounter God's presence in ways that honour their unique journeys.

In the Sacred Pause is an invitation to approach worship with both reverence and awareness. The liturgies draw on the solemnity of Holy Saturday but are intended for use throughout the liturgical year, providing a space for those grappling with the tensions between grief and hope.

The authors offer this work in the spirit of mutual support, recognising that trauma-informed care in worship is an ongoing and evolving practice. They hope that you will find creative ways to integrate this offering into your ministry, allowing it to become a source of solace and spiritual connection for those seeking safety within the sacred.

Acknowledgements

This book is the culmination of a collaborative journey shaped by faith, study and shared experiences. We extend our heartfelt gratitude to the ordinands who attended the first Theology and Trauma class taught by Dr Karen O'Donnell, as referenced in her Foreword. Your insights and participation profoundly influenced this work. Special thanks also go to the tutors of that course – Karen O'Donnell, Alison Gray, Will Rose-Moore, Robin Barden and Adam Scott – whose guidance and expertise were invaluable.

Collectively, we wish to thank the Cambridge Theological Federation and Westcott House for providing the opportunity to study theology through this transformative lens. To Westcott House, we are especially grateful for its role in our formation, nurturing our understanding and application of theology in ministry.

Individually, we each offer thanks to those who have supported us on this journey:

Claire   *To my beautiful children, Will and Anna, as a reminder that nothing is out of your reach.*

Mary   *To Saida and Pamela, whose experiences illuminated the importance of alternative forms of prayer and encouraged me to find words they could use in their conversations with God.*

Dan   *To my family and friends, without whom this would not have been possible. Special thanks to my late Mom, my best friend in heaven, and to God for helping me to deal with my own trauma.*

Ian   *To Sam Tudor and Will Rose-Moore for their advice, candour and support, and to my co-authors for their dedication and camaraderie.*

We are deeply grateful to Christine and David at Canterbury Press for their publishing expertise and support. A special mention must go to Karen O'Donnell – your enthusiasm for trauma theology and unwavering commitment to helping us understand and apply it in ministry are truly inspiring. The work you do is life-changing, and we are privileged to have benefited from your guidance.

Finally, we acknowledge the broader community of Trauma Theology and those who continue to explore its implications for faith and ministry. This book is offered in the hope that it will serve as a resource for those navigating the complexities of trauma within their faith communities.

Foreword

by Karen O'Donnell

About a month into my PhD studies, one of my supervisors rec-ommended I read some of Serene Jones' work.[1] 'She's doing some interesting thinking around trauma' was the recommendation. It was an aside, a casual suggestion, but one that would change the course of my research, and probably my life too. A decade later, when I arrived to work at Westcott House, I was well known for being a theologian with a particular interest in trauma. The irony was that, while I had researched and spoken about trauma for many years, I had never had the opportunity to actually teach a class on trauma theology. The academic year of 2023–24 was the first time I had that chance, and I co-taught it with colleagues from within the Cambridge Theological Federation. The beauti-fully thought-out, richly theological and deeply pastoral liturgies you are going to read (and hopefully use!) in this volume are some of the products of this phenomenal first class in Theology and Trauma.

This brief introduction to these liturgies will position them as part of an ongoing development of the work of trauma theology. I start by attempting to offer some definitions of trauma. This is always tricky and so I have offered some of the ways we might notice trauma before turning to any kind of definition. I then discuss some of the ways trauma survivors might be involved in a task of post-traumatic remaking in the aftermath of their trauma.

Central to this project is the theological motif and liturgical day of Holy Saturday. These resources were originally designed for use on Holy Saturday – the day between Good Friday and Easter

Sunday, between the Cross and the Resurrection. But in Trauma Theology, Holy Saturday has become a theological motif that far outstrips the specific liturgical day in significance and in possibility. I summarise Shelly Rambo's work on Holy Saturday and how it has influenced much of the theological work within this field. Finally, I attempt to answer the question of liturgy. Why is liturgy such an important and integral part of work within trauma theology, such that this is a liturgical offering?

What is Trauma?

We begin, as one always must when coming to speak of trauma, with the slipperiness and difficulties of trying to pin down what trauma is. We use the word casually in contemporary language. But trauma has some quite specific meanings that should ring-fence it for talking about specific kinds of responses to experiences.

Unpredictable

There is no such thing as a traumatic event. There may be events that we *expect* to be traumatic but no event is ontologically traumatic. There are only traumatic experiences of events. That is to say that two people might go through the exact same event and only one of them exhibit symptoms of a trauma response; only one of them experience this as a trauma. This diversity of experience is down to many factors including genetics and psychology. However it makes clear the fact that we cannot know what people will experience as traumatic.

Embodied

Bessel van der Kolk – the renowned trauma expert psychiatrist and author of *The Body Keeps the Score* – reminds us saliently that while talking therapies are a good thing for trauma survivors, they will only take us so far. He writes:

We have learned that trauma is not just an event that took place sometime in the past; it is also the imprint left by that experience on the mind, brain, and body ... Trauma results in a fundamental reorganisation of the way mind and brain manage perceptions. It changes not only how we think and what we think about, but also our very capacity to think. We have discovered that helping victims of trauma find the words to describe what has happened to them is profoundly meaningful, but usually it is not enough. The act of telling the story doesn't necessarily alter the automatic physical and hormonal responses of the bodies that remain hyper vigilant, prepared to be assaulted or violated at any time. For real change to take place, the body needs to learn that the danger has passed and live in the reality of the present.[2]

For post-traumatic remaking to take place, we must pay attention to the body. This underlines the fact that trauma is an embodied thing. We often think of it as something ethereal that sits loosely in the brain but trauma is something we can see throughout the whole body, from brain scans that show different parts of the brain working or not working due to a trauma response, to raised levels of hormones in the blood stream, to physiological responses such as raised blood pressure, panic attacks, emotional dysregulation – to name just a few. This embodied experience of trauma is part of what separates it from more prosaic responses to difficulties in life that we might call 'suffering'. Thinking about trauma requires one to hold a sense of holistic embodiedness, i.e. that the body is a complete, holistic entity of which the mind is a part. Resisting ancient forms of dualism between the mind and body, prevalent in many forms of Christian speech even today, means committing to the unity of the person.

Rupturing

There are many different ways of talking about what impact a trauma experience has on a person. My own preference is to talk about trauma causing three ruptures in a person. The first is a rupture in bodily integrity. This is the shattering of the idea that the body is a safe place. It might be very obvious if the trauma involves an injury to the flesh but it might also be less visible. If one considers more chronic forms of trauma, for example, the experience of coercive control, there is less likely to be an injury to the flesh but perhaps to the psyche. This is where that sense of holistic embodiment becomes even more significant. Regardless of the specific trauma event, the experience is one of rupturing bodily integrity.

The second rupture is that of time. The trauma survivor often finds that their sense of time and of timelines becomes confused and incoherent. Often a trauma survivor will struggle to accurately retell a narrative of what has happened to them because the timeline is jumbled and there may be gaps in their recollections. Trauma survivors' memories can be troublesome things. The past trauma event continually tries to invade the present through nightmares, flashbacks and hallucinations.

The final rupture is that of language and cognition. I link these two together because it is through language that we are able to make sense of who we are in the world. Thus, if language is ruptured, then cognition is ruptured too. The trauma survivor will often struggle to find the language to express what has happened to them or how they are feeling. They may find that this rupturing of language separates and isolates them from loved ones, unable to communicate because they may not know themselves what they want to say.

Of course, to present trauma in terms of these three ruptures is to tell only part of the story. While they are helpful to categorise some of what the trauma survivor is experiencing, they do not tell the whole story of such an experience. However, they are a helpful starting point from which to think about trauma and to differentiate it from other forms of negative life experience that we might name as suffering.

Defining Trauma

It might have seemed more logical to put this section on defining trauma at the beginning. However, one needs to understand something of the complexities of trauma before one can consider what it might mean to define trauma, to try and pin it down. Shelly Rambo refers to trauma as 'the suffering that doesn't go away'.[3] She helps make the point about the longevity and persistence of trauma but in my opinion, to name it as another form of suffering does injustice to the intensely embodied experience of trauma. Lucy Bond and Stef Craps start to get close to the perplexing and dynamic nature of trauma in their definition:

> Trauma, then, is slippery: blurring the boundaries between mind and body, memory and forgetting, speech and silence. It traverses the internal and the external, the private and the public, the individual and the collective. Trauma is dynamic: its parameters are endlessly shifting as it moves across disciplines and institutions, ages and cultures. Trauma is contested: its rhetoric, its origins, its symptoms, and its treatment have been subject to more than 150 years of controversy and debate.[4]

After Trauma

In some senses, there is no after with trauma. Trauma survivors will often live with the realities and impacts of their trauma experiences for their lifetimes. It is, as Rambo notes, the suffering that doesn't go away. I am reluctant to use words like 'healing' or 'recovery' in the way I talk about the life and work of the trauma survivor following such an experience. From a Christian perspective, 'healing' is a loaded term that comes with a lot of baggage and expectations about what God might do for a person (or not). And 'recovery' has a backward-looking sense that does not resonate with the experience of the trauma survivor – they cannot go back to who they were before the trauma experience. There is no return.

I prefer to use language of post-traumatic remaking of the self.

This gives a clearer picture of the work of the trauma survivor in the ongoing aftermath of their trauma experience. They are in a process of remaking themselves. This will be an iterative process that some may undertake for the rest of their lives. The English language requires us to present information in straight lines. However, the process of post-traumatic remaking is not linear. Therefore, while I am going to list elements of this remaking here, the order does not imply any kind of hierarchy or chronology.

This work of post-traumatic remaking needs to happen in a place of safety. It cannot be undertaken while the body is still at risk. This might be something that needs recurrent attention throughout a lifetime, especially as we know that trauma survivors might often put themselves at further risk through dysregulated behaviours. Constant and ongoing attention to the safety of the body as a necessity for engaging in this remaking is required.

The remaking will often involve some narration of the trauma experience. Knowing what we do about the impact of trauma on memory, this might be a laborious, ongoing task that requires many tellings in order to find any kind of sense of coherence. Such a narrative needs to be witnessed and believed. The narrative of the trauma survivor must be validated. We tend to think of this as lying on the therapist's couch talking but it could just as easily take forms of artwork and creative re-tellings that are articulated through the body of the trauma survivor and witnessed by their audience.

Trauma survivors often isolate themselves from friends and family. Trauma makes people feel alone and lonely. A key part of this remaking activity is reconnecting with community. This might be gradually rebuilding relationships, but it might also mean letting some relationships go as part of being in a place of safety and forming new relationships. For those who experienced their trauma within the Church, for example in the form of spiritual abuse, it might mean finding a new church or not going to church at all and finding community elsewhere. Increasingly, groups that function to provide this kind of Christian community do exist, as survivors' groups, advocacy groups, informal communities on social media. We must not be quick to disparage these kinds of communities; they might be exactly what a survivor needs.

Throughout all this, of course, it is essential to pay attention to one's body. Serene Jones talks about her need to find 'liturgies of the flesh' in her search for ways of attending to her body after her own trauma experiences. Ironically, she did not find these in the Church but rather in practices of yoga, breathwork, acupuncture and massage. There's no right prescription for this traumatised body; the survivor will find their own ways of paying attention to their flesh.

Holy Saturday

The field of Trauma Theology is still relatively nascent. Tracing its origins to some of the work done immediately post 9/11, it is a twenty-first-century endeavour. I began working in the field in 2013 and there were only a handful of scholars producing work in this discipline. I am delighted to have seen the field burgeon over the last decade. However, throughout all these wonderful new publications, one motif, one theological concept, has retained a central status. It is Shelly Rambo's work on Holy Saturday, from which this collection of liturgies has taken its inspiration.

Rambo highlights the way in which we – Christians, theologians, preachers, worship leaders – rush from the horror of the cross on Good Friday to the victory of the resurrection on Easter Sunday paying little attention to the space in between these two. She writes:

> Insofar as resurrection is proclaimed as life conquering or life victorious over death, it does not speak to the realities of traumatic suffering. In fact, one must recognize the ways in which resurrection proclamations may gloss over and negate the difficult experience of life in the aftermath of death ... The rush to life can belie the realities of death in life.[5]

Rambo points to Holy Saturday – the day between the cross and the resurrection – as a site of particular significance for Trauma Theology. Here we find a place in which the linear pattern of life-death-life is interrupted. There is a complicated mingling of death and life in Holy Saturday. Rambo draws this place of Holy Saturday into dialogue with the theme of witnessing – so important to the trauma survivor – as she examines the Johannine Gospel narratives of the disciples' experiences after the crucifixion. Here there is no hope. The disciples do not know that Jesus will be resurrected. They only know that their friend has died in a brutally cruel way. There is not yet the hope of the resurrection. Here Rambo places the 'interstitial figure of the Spirit'.[6] Rambo reminds us that while the Spirit is often connected to life because of the ways we commonly read the act of God breathing life into Adam in Genesis 2, the Spirit is more complex than that. As well as being the Spirit of life, the Spirit is also the Spirit of death. On the cross, at His moment of death, Jesus gives up His breath. The connection with Genesis 2 enables Rambo to read the Spirit as one of death as well as life. This Spirit is a complex, mingled and provocative encounter with both death and life. It is this Spirit that remains and witnesses on Holy Saturday, even when it seems impossible to conceive of any divine presence in the midst of trauma. Rather than a strong drive to life and victory, as also the Spirit of death, Rambo figures this Spirit as the one who sustains.[7]

Ritual and Liturgy in Trauma Theology

There's an ongoing joke that no matter where the Trauma Theologians begin their work, they will at some point end up talking about the Eucharist. Why? Because liturgies and trauma are both tangled up with bodies and memories and the Eucharist exemplifies this par excellence. Perhaps it's that liturgies seem to contain within them some of these post-traumatic remaking actions outline above.[8] Or it is that liturgies offer some sort of respite from the chaos of trauma. Or perhaps it is just that for people for whom repetition of the trauma experience has come to play such a crucial role in their lives, here is a repetition that brings peace. Whatever the reason, the ritual repetition found within liturgical practice has tremendous power and possibility, as yet under-explored.

We might consider, for example, the desire for ritual and liturgy that accompanies Remembrance Sunday. The rituals involved give meaning, draw communities together in both sorrow and hope, and may bring some sense of peace to those who remain. Or we might consider the service of Compline, a powerful liturgy for trauma survivors, for whom the night is a place of fear and nightmares. The service of Compline offers a ritual liturgical space for the trauma survivor to address their fears and find peace. I have written extensively about the need for the provision of ritual liturgical spaces for those who have experienced pregnancy loss, recognising that ritual in this case might help to bring a sense of completion and comfort to those whose journey toward parenthood has been disrupted.[9] Ritual liturgical offerings have a profound role to play in the work of post-traumatic remaking that the trauma survivor embarks upon. This new volume contributes tremendously to that provision, meeting a genuine unfilled need within the Christian community.

The Theology and Trauma Class

The original task the students in the Theology and Trauma class undertook for their assessment was a group project in which they had to produce a set of resources for a Holy Saturday liturgy that were trauma-oriented and trauma-informed. It is a version of these liturgies that you have here in this volume. They were originally written to take place on Holy Saturday but have, quite rightly, been broadened to be used in a range of 'holy Saturday' moments: places in which there is not yet hope but only sadness, brokenness and death mixing with life. These may be the places in which the trauma survivor finds themselves.

I am very proud of Claire, Dan, Ian and Mary, who have worked so hard to produce liturgies that are exactly what the Church needs. They will be a great gift to the Church. These four students are just a small representation of the class of students who took that first Theology and Trauma class, all of whom were preparing for ordained ministry. They were one of the best classes I've ever taught, and the Church will be the richer, the more compassionate, and the more informed because of these wonderful people and the learning in which they have engaged.

Notes

1 Serene Jones, 2009, *Trauma and Grace: Theology in a Ruptured World*, Louisville, KY: Westminster John Knox Press.

2 Bessel van der Kolk, 2015, *The Body Keeps the Score: Mind, Brain and Body in the Transformation of Trauma*, London: Penguin, p. 21.

3 Shelly Rambo, 2010, *Spirit and Trauma: A Theology of Remaining*, Louisville, KY: Westminster John Knox Press, p. 15.

4 Lucy Bond and Stef Craps, 2020, *Trauma*, London and New York: Routledge, p. 5.

5 Rambo, *Spirit and Trauma*, p. 7.

6 Rambo, *Spirit and Trauma*, p. 12.

7 Rambo's pneumatology is beautifully explored liturgically in Section F of this volume.

8 See here my own work on this in Karen O'Donnell, 2018, *Broken Bodies: The Eucharist, Mary and the Body in Trauma Theology*, London: SCM Press.

9 Karen O'Donnell, 2022, *The Dark Womb: Re-Conceiving Theology through Reproductive Loss*, London: SCM Press.

Introduction

In the solemn observance of Holy Saturday, we are invited into a space of reflection that sits uniquely at the heart of the Christian narrative – between the profound grief of Good Friday and the joy of Easter Sunday. This day, which we have characterised by several 'Themes', offers a profound opportunity for contemplation and connection. However, it also requires a sensitive and thoughtful approach, especially when we consider the potential for varied experiences of trauma within our congregations.

As a practical resource, *In the Sacred Pause* has been developed with a trauma-informed and trauma-oriented perspective at its core, aiming to create a liturgical space (for all) that honours the complexity of traumatic experiences. Trauma-informed care recognises the widespread impact of trauma and understands potential paths for remaking; it seeks to avoid re-traumatisation while promoting safe environments. In the context of Holy Saturday worship, this means crafting services that acknowledge the space people are presently in, including their pain and suffering, without assuming uniformity in how we *may* experience trauma.

While this book is rooted in the context of Holy Saturday, its themes and liturgies extend far beyond a single day in the liturgical calendar. The reality of Holy Saturday, with its tension between grief and hope, resonates throughout our lives and across the year. In many ways, we live in a perpetual Holy Saturday – where the trauma and pain of Good Friday linger as an ever-present reality, and we are constantly awaiting the renewal of Easter Day. Therefore, the reflections and practices contained within *In the Sacred Pause* are designed to be relevant and meaningful at any time, offering a compassionate space for contemplation, healing and spiritual connection whenever your community may need it.

As a resource, this work uses language and statements that reflect an understanding of trauma's impacts and is trauma-oriented. The content is developed to offer flexibility, allowing leaders to adapt materials to suit the specific needs and spiritual atmosphere of their community. This approach respects the diversity of congregational experiences, ensuring that worship is a place where all can feel seen, heard and supported in their spiritual journey. Much of its content is taken from authorised forms of worship but, where it has been created specifically for this resource, we offer it for use under Canon B5.

Creating a supportive environment for those attending trauma-oriented services is paramount. As such, this resource encourages a sense of shared journeying and mutual support within the community, recognising that any potential for remaking often happens in the context of relationships and shared spaces. We aim to foster an atmosphere of compassion, understanding and openness, where the sacredness of each person's experience is honoured.

Additionally, we acknowledge that, while spiritual practices and affirmations can offer significant comfort and support, they are not substitutes for professional psychological care. It is crucial to encourage individuals dealing with trauma to seek and continue professional counselling and support alongside their spiritual practices. This resource emphasises the importance of voluntary engagement, allowing individuals to interact with the material in ways that feel most comfortable and beneficial for them, without any pressure.

As you turn the pages of *In the Sacred Pause*, we invite you to do so with a heart open to the nuances of human experience.

Despite knowing that the dawn of Easter awaits us, we have striven to hold the sacred space of Holy Saturday in our hearts, allowing the grace found in contemplating on this day to shape us as we continue our spiritual journey, grounded in the assurance of God's unfailing presence with us, every day, and every step of the way.

Resource Themes

In this resource, Themes are used to guide leaders in the creation of liturgies for Holy Saturday.

On Holy Saturday, we believe we are invited to dwell in a moment of deep contemplation, a pause in the liturgical rhythm that calls us to reflect on the mysteries of faith. In this space, we are not alone: we are accompanied by the weight of history, the presence of the divine and the shared humanity of our community. We have chosen these Themes – silence and presence, waiting, darkness, disorientation, community and witness, memory, vulnerability and lament – as guideposts for our journey, allowing them to speak into the depths of our experiences and to illuminate the path of our spiritual walk.

We have consciously decided not to begin this resource with biblical character narratives of 'trauma' because they were not written in ways that are trauma-informed, and there is a concern about potential triggers. Instead, we aim to prioritise trauma sensitivity and inclusivity. However, we acknowledge that it is important to balance this with the recognition that engagement with biblical characters, under careful and compassionate guidance, can also offer meaningful opportunities for connection.

We have decided that a 'middle ground' could involve offering multiple biblical pathways within the liturgy for engaging with trauma, including options for those who may find direct engagement with biblical narratives useful, alongside alternative thematic and expressive resources for those who may not.

We do not expect leaders to follow one Theme throughout the liturgy, although this is possible; instead leaders may wish to select elements that work well for their own context. While

Themes were developed as part of the initial thinking around Holy Saturday, they can be applied at any time.

The Themes

Silence and Presence: Formed by the stillness of Holy Saturday, we are invited into a profound silence, not as an absence, but as a sanctuary where God's presence is palpably near. This silence, whether experienced on Holy Saturday or any day of the year, asks us to listen – to the quiet stirrings of our hearts and the gentle whispers of the Divine – reminding us that in our most solitary moments, we are never truly alone.

Waiting: The essence of Holy Saturday lies in its sacred waiting – a liminal space where time seems suspended, and transformation occurs in the hidden depths of our being. This Theme extends beyond a single day, reminding us that spiritual growth often unfolds in the quiet anticipation of what is yet to be, shaping us in ways we may not fully understand until we emerge on the other side.

Darkness: Inviting us to sit with the discomfort of darkness, this Theme acknowledges it not as something to be feared but as a place where faith can be deepened. The darkness of Holy Saturday, symbolic of the grave but also the womb of the earth, serves as a reminder that in God's economy, even the darkest night can be a precursor to new life – a truth that remains relevant in all seasons of our spiritual journey.

Disorientation: Life's unexpected turns can leave us feeling lost and disoriented, much like the disciples on the day after the crucifixion. Holy Saturday embodies this sense of disorientation, inviting us to trust that even when the path ahead is unclear, we are held by a God who knows the way. This Theme resonates throughout our lives, reminding us that disorientation can be a sacred space where divine guidance emerges.

Community and Witness: Our journey through darkness and waiting is not a solitary endeavour. Holy Saturday reminds us of the power of community – to bear witness to each other's struggles, to offer support, and to find strength in shared silence. This call to recognise our interconnectedness and the communal aspect of our spiritual journeys is a timeless invitation, echoing throughout our lives.

Memory: In the reflective pause that Holy Saturday offers, we are encouraged to remember – to hold in our hearts – the stories of faith that have shaped us, the moments of grace that have sustained us, and the enduring faithfulness of God that has carried us through every season of life. This Theme invites us to engage with our memories as a source of strength and continuity in our ongoing spiritual walk while recognising that a trauma survivor may not be able to remember clearly.

Vulnerability: Embracing vulnerability on Holy Saturday means acknowledging our wounds, doubts and fears before God; we trust that in our openness, we are met with divine love and grace. This recognition of our shared humanity, exemplified by Jesus, draws us closer to the heart of the Divine not just on this day, but whenever we are willing to be vulnerable in our faith journey.

Lament: Holy Saturday gives us permission to lament – to express our sorrow, confusion and longing without reservation. Lament, as a powerful form of prayer, transcends any single day, serving as a testament to the depth of our faith and reminding us that even in the shadow of death, we are heard by a God who weeps with us.

These Themes, though inspired by the profound silence, presence, darkness and disorientation of Holy Saturday, offer a timeless framework for encountering the divine mystery that permeates all of life. In the shared experience of community, memory, vulnerability and lament, we weave together a tapestry of faith that holds our sorrows and hopes in tension, offering guidance and comfort throughout the entire liturgical year.

Liturgy Building Blocks

This resource offers structured guidance for incorporating the Themes into several building blocks for your service. From the 'Gathering and Greeting' to the 'Service Ending', each section is crafted with mindfulness towards creating a space that honours the complexity of human emotion and the mystery of faith.

Below is a brief introduction to the key 'blocks' of the service, designed to support you in creating a meaningful and reflective worship experience.

A: Gathering and Greeting

Begin your service by setting a tone of welcome and solemnity, inviting participants into a shared space of contemplation and community.

B: Penitence

Engage with the themes of reflection and self-examination, providing an opportunity for attendees to acknowledge their frailties in a supportive environment. We include a variety of wording from which the worship leader may choose to suit their context.

C: Liturgy of the Word

Use carefully selected Scripture readings that resonate with any chosen Theme, encouraging deep reflection on God's presence in times of silence and waiting.

D: Psalms and Canticles

Utilising the Psalms and Canticles to give voice to the communal and individual expressions of lament, praise and longing is a useful part of a trauma-oriented/informed service, and these are often context-specific.

E: Creeds and Affirmations of Faith

Offer affirmations that emphasise the Trinitarian nature of our faith while respecting the context of your setting allowing for a profession of faith that acknowledges the complexities of the human and divine experience.

F: Prayers and Movement

Incorporate prayers that articulate any chosen Theme, and seek to provide space for personal and communal petitions and intercessions. Movements that embody the Themes can invite a physical expression of the liturgy which may be useful in some contexts.

G: Praise and Thanksgiving

To the glory of God. Even in a context of solemnity, moments of praise and thanksgiving acknowledge the constant presence and sovereignty of God. (This may offer some more nuance to worship.) This section includes suggested hymns and songs which are optional to include in any worship.

H: Secular Alternatives

We have provided several secular alternatives, along with a rationale for their selection, that could be used in place of hymns, songs, canticles or prayers.

I: Ending the Service

Conclude your service in a way that honours the journey through one of the Themes (where a Theme has been used).

Prayers of Absolution are not offered within this resource for the reasons outlined in the Appendix.

Warnings and Considerations

The authors wish to ensure that some basic principles are considered when using these resources.

Contextual flexibility

We ask that you recognise the diversity of your congregation, including the varied experiences of trauma and loss. These resources are designed to be versatile, allowing you to select those that best fit the specific needs and spiritual atmosphere of your community.

Creating a supportive environment

Please ensure that the environment in which the Building Blocks are shared is one of compassion, understanding and openness. Encourage a sense of shared journeying and mutual support within the community. Be mindful of how Themes could be perceived in context to avoid unintentional misuse.

Sensitivity to trauma

Be aware that the Themes of darkness, disorientation, silence and waiting, while theologically rich, might resonate differently with individuals, especially those with experiences of trauma. Some might find these Themes challenging or triggering. Approach the use of these resources with sensitivity and a readiness to provide support.

Not a substitute for professional care

Emphasise that while spiritual practices and worship in any form can offer significant comfort and support, they are not substitutes for professional psychological care. Encourage individuals dealing with trauma to seek and continue professional counselling and support alongside their spiritual practices.

Voluntary engagement

Make it clear that engagement with these resources is entirely voluntary. Individuals should feel free to engage with them in a way that feels most comfortable to them, without any pressure to participate in a manner that might feel re-traumatising or uncomfortable.

Pastoral follow-up

Offer pastoral follow-up for individuals who may find certain aspects particularly stirring or difficult. Make it known that your pastoral care team is available for conversation, prayer and support.

Avoid presumption of universal experience

Recognise that not everyone will relate to the Themes in the same way. Offer multiple entry points into the worship experience, allowing individuals to engage at their own comfort level.

Balance in Theme presentation

While it is important to delve into Holy Saturday's solemn Themes, please ensure that there is a balance that respects the required liturgy for the context without leading the congregation into despair. The goal is to create a space for contemplation which is safe and reverent. Section F may offer suggestions as to how to do this, as does the section 'Some other Planning Considerations'.

Abbreviations of Sources

CCP   *Celebrating Common Prayer*
CWDP   *Common Worship: Daily Prayer*
CWTS   *Common Worship: Times and Seasons*
NPP   *New Parish Prayers*
NPW   *New Patterns of Worship*
TRL   *The Rhythm of Life: Celtic Daily Prayer*

The Liturgies

A: Gathering and Greeting

Pastoral Introduction

As we meet in the solemnity of Holy Saturday, we acknowledge that we bring our own stories and experiences, and that sometimes these can be burdensome and heavy. We aim to create a space that is reflective, prayerful and above all, safe for everyone. Therefore, for the purpose of this service, we will not share 'the peace' in its traditional form as we recognise that this space might be one that does not include explicit interaction with others as we move through the liturgy. There is, however, a form of peace included in this section that can be offered as a greeting.

Purpose of the Gathering and Greeting

Both clearly mark that the service has begun and can set the tone of the service. A brief introduction and personal welcome can be offered by the leader before or after the greeting. We strongly recommend that during the gathering and greeting, the leader makes it clear where pastoral support can be sought during the service and afterwards. You may wish to use one of the following greetings:

A1   Welcome in the name of Christ:
God's grace, mercy and peace be with you
and also with you.

NPW, A2

A2 The grace and mercy of our Lord Jesus Christ be with you
and also with you.

NPW, A3

A3 The Lord be with you
and also with you.
Let us worship God.

NPW, A11

A4 We come from scattered lives to meet with God.
Let us recognise His presence with us.

Silence is kept

As God's people we have gathered:
let us worship Him together.

NPW, A12

A5 We meet in the name of God:
Father, Son and Holy Spirit.

NPW, A19

A6 We meet in the presence of God
**who knows our needs,
hears our cries,
feels our pain,
and heals our wounds.**

NPW, A34

A7 The peace of the Lord be always with you
and also with you.

NPW, H5

B: Penitence

Some of the liturgies in this section are taken from *New Patterns of Worship* and *New Parish Prayers*, while others were created by the authors.

You are also welcome and invited to write your own confession, reflecting on the Themes of this resource, individually or as a community.

In preparing this resource, we acknowledge the fact that some of the language used in this section might be triggering for some people (e.g. guilt, brokenness, sin). As a trauma-oriented and trauma-informed liturgy, this resource is created to be suitable for the whole Church community and, as you can see in the Introduction, there is rationale for offering these in that completeness.

Prayers of Absolution are not offered within this section for the reasons outlined in the Appendix.

B1 INVITATION TO CONFESSION

B1.1   'Holy, holy, holy is the Lord God Almighty.'
We long for the fire of God's cleansing to touch
   our unclean lips,
for our guilt to be removed and our sin wiped out.
So we meet Father, Son and Holy Spirit with repentance
   in our heart.

cf Isaiah 6 and Revelation 4
NPW, B4

B1.2 Human sin disfigures the whole creation,
which groans with eager longing for God's redemption.
We confess our sin in penitence and faith.

cf Romans 8.22, 23
NPW, B6

B1.3 When the Lord comes,
He will bring to light the things now hidden in darkness,
and will disclose the purposes of the heart.
Therefore, in the light of Christ let us confess our sins.

NPW, B7

B1.4 God shows His love for us in that,
while we were still sinners, Christ died for us.
Let us then show our love for Him by confessing
our sins in penitence and faith.

cf Romans 5.8
NPW, B12

B1.5 The sacrifice of God is a broken spirit;
a broken and contrite heart God will not despise.
Let us come to the Lord, who is full of compassion,
and acknowledge our transgressions in penitence
and faith.

cf Psalm 51.17
NPW, B21

B1.6 The sacrifice acceptable to God is a broken spirit;
a broken and contrite heart God will not despise.
Our sins accuse us. We confess them to God.

cf Psalm 51.17
NPW, B20

B1.7   Compassion and forgiveness belong to the Lord our God,
though we have rebelled against Him.
Let us then renounce our wilfulness and ask His mercy
by confessing our sins in penitence and faith.

cf Daniel 9.9
NPW, B22

B1.8   Christ Himself bore our sins in His body on the cross
so that,
free from sin, we might live for righteousness;
by His wounds we have been healed.
Let us confess our sins.

cf 1 Peter 2.24
NPW, B23

B1.9   Beloved community, as we abide in the solemnity
of this day,
we may find ourselves in a place of profound
uncertainty and reflection,
reminiscent of the disciples' vigil.
We are invited to pause and dwell in this liminal space,
where light has not yet pierced the shadow.
Let us confess our sins as an act of trust in the God who
walks with us through every darkness,
every moment of waiting, and every season of
disorientation.

B1.10   In the quiet of this this day,
we stand at the threshold of reflection and renewal.
As we navigate the spaces between our sorrows
and our hopes,
we approach the Divine with honesty,
laying bare the burdens of our hearts.
In a spirit of penitence, we open ourselves
to the grace of God,
who meets us in our most profound moments
of silence and waiting.

B1.11 In the sacred pause of this day,
we are reminded of the complexities of our humanity –
caught between the now and the not yet.
We come before God, not with haste but with humility,
acknowledging our vulnerabilities, our doubts and our
yearnings for clarity and direction.
In this solemn space, we offer our confession,
trusting in God's endless mercy.

B1.12 As we dwell in the mystery of this day,
we recognise the invitation to introspection
and the call to acknowledge our shortcomings.
In the embrace of this day's profound stillness,
may we find the courage to face our own shadows,
confessing with the assurance that God's presence is a
constant source of comfort and guidance,
even in our moments of deepest uncertainty.

B2: CONFESSION

B2.1 Lord Jesus Christ, we confess that we have failed You
as did Your first disciples.
We ask for Your mercy and Your help.

Our selfishness betrays You:
Lord, forgive us.
Christ have mercy.
We fail to share the pain of Your suffering:
Lord, forgive us.
Christ have mercy.
We run away from those who abuse You:
Lord, forgive us.
Christ have mercy.
We are afraid of being known to belong to You:
Lord, forgive us.
Christ have mercy.

NPW, B45

B2.2   Lord God,
we have sinned against You; we have done evil
   in Your sight.
We are sorry and repent.
Have mercy on us according to Your love.
Wash away our wrongdoing and cleanse us from our sin.
Renew a right spirit within us and restore us to the joy
   of Your salvation,
through Jesus Christ our Lord.
Amen.

cf Psalm 51
NPW, B48

B2.3   For turning away from You, and ignoring Your will
   for our lives;
Father, forgive us:
save us and help us.

For behaving just as we wish, without thinking of You;
Father, forgive us:
save us and help us.

For failing You by what we do and think and say;
Father, forgive us:
save us and help us.

For letting ourselves be drawn away from You by
   temptations in the world about us;
Father, forgive us:
save us and help us.

For living as if we were ashamed to belong to Your Son;
Father, forgive us:
save us and help us.

NPW, B49

B2.4   Almighty God,
long-suffering and of great goodness:
I confess to You, I confess with my whole heart
my neglect and forgetfulness of Your commandments,
my wrongdoing, thinking and speaking;
the hurts I have done to others,
and the good I have left undone.
O God, forgive me, for I have sinned against You;
and raise me to newness of life;
through Jesus Christ our Lord.
Amen.

NPW, B50

B2.5   My God, for love of You
I desire to hate and forsake all sins
by which I have ever displeased You;
and I resolve by the help of Your grace
to commit them no more;
and to avoid all opportunities to sin.
Help me to do this,
through Jesus Christ our Lord.
Amen.

NPW, B51

B2.6   O God, who is ever-present in the midst of our
deepest night,
we come before You in the stillness of this day, hearts
heavy and spirits sombre,
reflecting on the disciples' own bewilderment and
sorrow on that first Holy Saturday.

Pause for silent reflection

We confess, O Lord, that like them, we too find
ourselves disoriented by life's trials,
daunted by the shadows that linger, and perplexed by
the silences where we expect Your voice.

We admit our struggles, our quickness to despair, and
our slowness to remember Your steadfast presence in
all things.

Pause for silent reflection

In Your boundless mercy, meet us here in the depths of
our vulnerability.
Forgive us for our doubts, our fears, and the ways we
fail to trust in Your abiding love.
Grant us the grace to endure this time, to find solace in
the mystery,
and to hold space for our grief and confusion,
knowing that You, O God,
are with us in our waiting.

Give us the strength to embrace the discomfort of
not knowing,
and to find peace in the promise that You are God, even
in the silence, even in the darkness.

Help us to bear witness to each other's journeys,
to offer love where there is pain, and to extend grace
where there is faltering.

In this sacred pause,
renew our spirits and bind us together in the fellowship
of shared uncertainty,
that we may support one another.
Amen.

B2.7 God our Father, You have set forth the way of life for
us in Your beloved Son.
We confess with shame our slowness to learn of Him,
our failure to follow Him,
our reluctance to bear His cross.
Forgive, according to Your steadfast love,
the poverty of our worship,
our neglect of fellowship and the means of grace,
our hesitating witness for Christ,

our imperfect stewardship of Your gifts.
Have mercy upon us, O God;
cleanse us from our sins,
and put a new and right spirit within us;
for the sake of Jesus Christ our Saviour.
Amen.

NPP, 48

B2.8   Heavenly Father, we confess how often we disobey what
we know to be Your will;
how often we forget You and leave You out of our lives;
how often we are too blind to know our sins, too proud
to admit them,
too indifferent to make amends.
In Your mercy, O Lord, forgive us our sins,
and give us honest, humble and penitent hearts,
for the sake of our Saviour Jesus Christ.
Amen.

NPP, 48

B2.9   Almighty God, lover of all people, giver of all grace,
look mercifully upon us who acknowledge our sins;
create in us a pure heart and a steadfast spirit;
and lead us in the paths of holiness and righteousness;
through Jesus Christ our Lord.
Amen.

NPP, 49

B2.10   O God, who sent Your Son Jesus Christ to be the
Saviour of humankind:
teach us to know our sins and to turn from them;
show us what is our duty and help us to do it;
and so, lead us by Your Holy Spirit that we may walk in
the way of Your will;
through Jesus Christ our Lord.
Amen.

NPP, 50

B2.11 Gracious God, in the silence of this day,
we acknowledge the ways we have wandered from
Your path.
Our hearts have harboured doubt, our minds are
clouded by fear.
We confess that we have often overlooked Your
presence in our moments of despair and isolation.

Pause for silent reflection

We seek Your forgiveness, O Lord, for the times we
have failed to embody Your love.
Help us to recognise Your grace in the stillness of today.
Renew our spirits, that we may walk in faith even when
the way ahead is obscured.

Pause for silent reflection

In Your mercy, hear our prayer and knit us closer in the
bond of community,
that together we may bear witness to the strength found
in shared vulnerability
and the peace that comes from trusting in Your
unfailing love.
Amen.

B2.12 O Merciful God, today we stand in the gap between
sorrow and joy,
acknowledging our discomfort with the unknown and
our impatience for resolution.

We confess our struggle to remain present with You in
the discomfort of waiting,
our resistance to embracing the fullness of this
sacred pause.

Pause for silent reflection

Forgive us, Lord, for the moments we have rushed to
escape our uncertainties rather than sitting with
them, for the times we have let our fears overshadow
our faith.

Grant us the courage to endure the silence, and the
grace to find Your guiding presence in the midst of
our questions.

Pause for silent reflection

As we wait, help us to support one another with
compassion, to share the burdens of those around
us, and to discover the profound connections
that are forged in the shared spaces of our human
vulnerability.
Amen.

C: Liturgy of the Word

Purpose of the Readings

The suggested readings are offered with the aim of continuing to hold the grief of Good Friday, while also dwelling in the seemingly hopeless reality of Holy Saturday – a reality that we might experience at any point in our spiritual journey. The selected texts intentionally draw attention away from redemptive hope, and the material offered purposefully creates connections to the Themes of these resources. The Old Testament passages reflect a sense of God's people waiting and lamenting, while the New Testament narratives seek to remember and give voice to all that happened during the trial, execution and burial of Jesus, as well as the wider impact of these events. The readings aim to illustrate, particularly to trauma survivors, that God can simply be with us in the midst of extreme difficulty.

The passages have been selected with the NRSV version of the Bible in mind, but it may be appropriate to consider other translations, depending on your setting and context. Some further psalms can be found in Section D: Psalms and Canticles.

Gospel Accounts

The Gospel texts in this resource avoid the violence of the cross in recognition that these narratives can be deeply triggering to survivors of violent trauma, but they seek to draw on the wider story of both Holy Week and the liturgical year. It is recognised that for survivors of trauma, the re-telling of their story and finding language for their experience is a central tenet to potential remaking. It is acknowledged that, in the recounting of experience, the trauma often resists being remembered or represented. In response to this, some of the suggested Gospel readings are paired with other Gospel accounts that tell the same story, to offer multiple interpretations of the same narrative. Others are stand-alone narratives.

Sermons and Reflections

While sermons and reflections are an appropriate response to hearing the liturgy of the Word, in the context of this service we suggest that other responses might be more fitting. We suggest offering participants the space to make sense (for themselves) of the words they have received. This can be achieved simply by holding a silent and reflective space following the readings.

This reflective space helps the participants to make sense of the readings independently, rather than having thoughts and feelings imposed on them. If appropriate, you may want to offer a space to light a candle, or to use some of the resources from the 'Prayer and Movement' section of this resource (See Section F).

C1: SILENCE AND PRESENCE

Old Testament

1 Kings 19.11–12

The story of Elijah experiencing God not in the wind, earthquake or fire, but in a gentle whisper, underscoring the divine presence in silence.

Exodus 33.12–14

Moses asks God whom He will send with him to the Promised Land, and God tells him that His presence will go with him.

Ecclesiastes 3.1–8

A passage where we are reminded there is a season for everything, including a time to keep silent.

Habakkuk 2.20

A verse about keeping silent before the Lord in His holy Temple.

Isaiah 30.15

A verse affirming that quietness and trust is a source of strength.

Psalm

Psalm 62.1–2, 5–8

An affirmation that for the soul that waits in silence, God is a rock and a fortress.

New Testament

Luke 9.28–36

An account where three of the disciples are with Jesus when His full glory is revealed during the Transfiguration. Although they are told to keep quiet about these events, it is a holy and life-changing moment for them because they know that they are in the presence of the Messiah.

Mark 4.35–41

This passage tells the story of Jesus bringing peace and calm to the raging sea when He commands it to be still. The disciples are in awe that even the wind and the waves can be controlled by His presence.

Gospels

Luke 23.6–9; Matthew 27.11–14; Mark 15.4–5

The passage where Jesus is questioned at length by Herod/Pilate but says nothing. We simply hold this part of the story and offer it as a space to sit and be present in Jesus' quietness.

C2: WAITING

Old Testament

Isaiah 40.27–31

This text reminds the reader that those who wait for the Lord shall have their strength renewed.

1 Samuel 1.9–20

In this passage, Hannah had been hoping to conceive a child and, after she cries out in prayer, the Lord remembers her plea and she conceives a son. Hannah's despair is evident in the text as she waits.

Psalms

Psalm 27.14

The psalmist (David) expresses his confidence in God. In this verse the reader is encouraged to 'wait on the Lord'.

Psalm 40.1–2

A psalm written in the pit of despair, but where David describes his waiting. Even in David's despair, God hears his cry.

New Testament

Romans 8.22–25

Paul reminds us that we wait for what we do not see.

2 Peter 3.8–10

This text is offered to make the point that when we are waiting for something that is much needed or anticipated, time can feel like it has stood still. This passage reminds us that with the Lord, one day can feel like a thousand years and a thousand years can feel like a day. It is reminding us that God will fulfil His promises to us, in His own time.

James 5.7–8

These verses are about waiting, with patience, for the Lord's coming.

Hebrews 6.15

This verse remembers Abraham's patient wait for God's promise.

Luke 2.25–32

The story of Simeon, who waits for the consolation of Israel and whose patience is rewarded.

Gospels

Luke 9.28–36; Matthew 17.1–9; Mark 9.1–13

In this account, Jesus reveals His full glory to His disciples during the Transfiguration.

C3: DARKNESS

Old Testament

Genesis 1.1–5

The creation narrative demonstrates that God is present even in the darkness and chaos of the unformed earth.

1 Kings 19.3–7

We are told in this passage that Elijah feels desperate and alone (and is engulfed in a spiritual darkness). As he sits under a tree, an angel of the Lord meets him in his despair and offers him comfort. The angel is not afraid to dwell in the spiritual darkness of his companion.

Psalms

Psalm 23

This psalm is a well-known prayer of comfort and a reminder that even when we find ourselves in a place of darkness, we should not be fearful, for God is with us.

Psalm 88.1–8

A psalm of lament that does not shy away from darkness. The psalmist seeks God in the darkness, which makes the psalm a powerful reflection for Holy Saturday.

Psalm 121

A psalm of comfort as we remember that God watches over us while we are awake and asleep, for God neither slumbers nor sleeps.

New Testament

John 1.1–5

A verse that focuses on the reminder that even though there is darkness, Jesus (the Light of the world) still shines.

Luke 22.39–43

A brief extract from the scene in the Garden of Gethsemane where Jesus prays to God in despair.

Gospels

Matthew 27.45–46; Mark 15.33–34; Luke 23.44–46

This section of Scripture reminds us that as Jesus gives up His spirit in death, a darkness falls over the whole land. We also sit in this darkness on Holy Saturday, or at times when we find ourselves in seemingly hopeless situations.

C4: DISORIENTATION

Old Testament

Genesis 1

In this well-known chapter, God brings order to disorder in the creation narrative.

Job 23.8–10

This text describes Job searching for God in disorientation and pain.

Psalms

Psalm 8

A psalm that echoes the theme of beauty emerging from the depths of creation. This psalm would work well with Genesis 1 as the Old Testament text.

Psalm 137.1–6

This psalm captures the disorientation and sorrow of the Israelites in Babylon, reflecting on the challenge of maintaining faith in a foreign land.

New Testament

John 11.17–27

In this account, Martha affirms her faith in Christ as the one who can do what seems impossible, even in the midst of her grief and disorientation.

Luke 8.22–25

A story where Jesus calms the raging storm.

Gospel

Luke 24.13–35

This passage tells the story of Jesus meeting with the disciples on the road to Emmaus. In this account, the disciples' disorientation turns to recognition in the breaking of bread. This story subtly outlines the journey from confusion to understanding.

C5: COMMUNITY AND WITNESS

Old Testament

Ruth 1.1–18

The story of Ruth and Naomi is a demonstration of loyalty, and it exemplifies the significance of community in the Hebrew Bible.

Psalm

Psalm 133

This is a psalm of praise about the delights of living in unity with others.

New Testament

Acts 2.42–47

This passage depicts the early Christian community's life of fellowship, prayer and shared resources, emphasising the strength and witness of community.

Acts 4.32–33

In this Biblical account, early Jesus followers live in community and share everything they have.

Hebrews 10.24–25

These verses remind us to encourage one another in love.

John 13.34–35

This is a well-known passage which reminds us of Jesus' commandment to love one another as He has loved us, highlighting the essence of Christian community and witness.

Romans 12.4–5

This Pauline account reminds us that the body of Christ is made up of many members, yet is still one body.

Gospel

John 19.25–27

This scene is taken at the foot of the cross where those whom Jesus loves are gathered. Jesus ensures His mother will be cared for after His death, providing community once He is gone.

C6: MEMORY

Old Testament

Deuteronomy 8.2–3, 11–18

This reading encourages the hearers to remember the Lord and His commandments, especially His provision during times of wandering in the wilderness.

Isaiah 46.8–11

These verses remember the former things of old.

Psalms

Psalm 105.1–5

This psalm speaks of God's faithfulness to Israel, with the psalmist speaking of seeking the Lord, His strength and His presence continually.

Psalm 143.1–6

This psalm is a cry of lament and the psalmist is remembering their afflictions. There is a desperation in its tone, and it does not conclude with any sense of clear answer to prayer.

New Testament

1 Corinthians 11.23–26

In this passage of Scripture, Paul reminds the community in Corinth that what was received from the Lord is also to be passed on to others.

2 Timothy 1.1–6

This extract from the book of Timothy offers an example of thanksgiving and encouragement, remembering the lived faith of those who went before.

Gospels

Matthew 26.26–29; Luke 22.19–20; Mark 14.22–25

This is an account of the Last Supper, where Jesus commands the disciples to 'do this in remembrance of me', focusing on the act of remembering as central to faith.

C7: VULNERABILITY

Old Testament

1 Samuel 1.9–20

In this passage from Samuel, we learn of Hannah (who is unable to conceive) displaying a willingness to be vulnerable before God, crying out in prayer despite her distress and bitter weeping.[1]

Ruth 1.1–18

This is an account of Ruth and Naomi, who place themselves in a vulnerable position when they arrive together as widows in a foreign place. Their story is testament to them finding strength in their vulnerability together.

Isaiah 53.3–4

This passage from Isaiah offers a prefiguring of Christ who becomes vulnerable on our behalf.

Psalms

Psalm 34.17–20

This psalm highlights God's attentiveness to the righteous, especially in their brokenness; God saves those with a contrite spirit.

Psalm 62.5–8

A psalm which reminds us that God is our rock and our salvation, and you can pour your heart out to Him.

Psalm 143.1–6

This psalm is a cry of lament where the psalmist does not hold back in making themselves vulnerable by bringing all their sorrow before God.

New Testament

John 4.1–42

The woman at the well makes herself vulnerable in the dialogue she shares with Jesus. In making herself vulnerable, she encounters Jesus in a powerful and life-changing way.

Mark 10.46–52

Bartimaeus is vulnerable and desperate for Jesus to help him. He calls out despite some ordering him to be quiet. Jesus, on encountering him, acknowledges both his vulnerability and faith and responds with tenderness and grace.

Hebrews 4.15–16

In this letter to the Hebrews, we are reminded that Jesus understands us in our weakness.

Romans 8.26–27

In this letter to the Romans, we are told that the Spirit helps us in our weakness and vulnerability.

2 Corinthians 12.9–10

This text is Paul's reflection on strength made perfect in weakness and finding contentment in vulnerabilities for Christ's sake.

Gospel

Matthew 11.28–30

In this passage from Matthew, we are promised that Jesus gives rest to those who carry heavy burdens.

C8: LAMENT

Old Testament

Lamentations 3.19–33

This passage reflects a personal and communal lament but also a hope in God's steadfast love and mercy, emphasising His sovereignty, even in suffering.

Psalms

Psalm 22

This psalm demonstrates a profound expression of feeling forsaken by God, yet the psalm also recalls God's faithfulness.

Psalm 130.1–2

In this psalm, the psalmist calls out to God from the depths of despair.

Psalm 42.1–8

This psalm speaks of longing for God.

Psalm 88.1–6

This psalm is a song of lament.

New Testament

Romans 8.37–39

This letter to the Romans reminds us that whatever challenges we face, nothing can separate us from the love of God.

Revelation 21.3–4

In the book of Revelation we find the promise that there will be a time when God will wipe away every tear from our eye.

Gospel

John 11.32–36

This passage tells of the story of Lazarus. On hearing of the death of His friend Lazarus, Jesus wept.

Note

1 Karen O'Donnell, 2019, *Broken Bodies: The Eucharist, Mary and the Body in Trauma Theology*, SCM Press, p. 103.

D: Psalms and Canticles

Purpose of the Readings

Praying with Psalms of Lament has been a longstanding tradition in Ancient Israel and throughout Christian history. Despite their lack of popularity in some contemporary worship, we believe that these psalms offer a meaningful method for prayer and reflection on the Themes presented in this resource. Suitable for each Theme, the Psalms of Lament, or selected verses from them, can deepen your engagement.

Below, we provide a selection of these psalms, each linked to specific themes for focused reflection. Additional psalms can be found in the Bible Readings section. We warmly encourage you to compose your own psalm, particularly as you contemplate the Theme of Lament. To aid in this process, we provide a template below.

D1: PSALMS

Psalms of lament

Please note that the authors have used thematic titles for these psalms to aid in your choice. Please check the contextual suitability of each psalm chosen.

Psalm 3: 'Trust in God under adversity'
Psalm 4: 'Confident plea for deliverance from enemies'
Psalm 5: 'Prayer for protection from the wicked'
Psalm 6: 'Prayer for mercy in time of trouble'

Psalm 7: 'Prayer for vindication'
Psalm 9: 'Thanksgiving for God's justice'
Psalm 10: 'Prayer for deliverance from enemies'
Psalm 12: 'Plea for help in evil times'
Psalm 13: 'Trust in the salvation of the Lord'
Psalm 14: 'The folly and wickedness of humankind'
Psalm 17: 'Prayer for deliverance from persecutors'
Psalm 22: 'Plea for deliverance from suffering and hostility'
Psalm 25: 'Prayer for guidance and protection'
Psalm 26: 'Plea for justice and declaration of righteousness'
Psalm 27: 'Triumphant song of confidence'
Psalm 28: 'Prayer for help and thanksgiving for it'
Psalm 31: 'Prayer and praise for deliverance from enemies'
Psalm 32: 'The joy of forgiveness'
Psalm 38: 'Prayer of a suffering penitent'
Psalm 39: 'Prayer for wisdom and forgiveness'
Psalm 41: 'Assurance of God's help and a plea for healing'
Psalm 42: 'Longing for God and His help in distress'
Psalm 43: 'Prayer for deliverance'
Psalm 44: 'National lament and prayer for help'
Psalm 51: 'Prayer for cleansing and pardon'
Psalm 52: 'Denunciation of a Doeg-like character'
Psalm 53: 'The folly of denying God'
Psalm 54: 'Prayer for vindication'
Psalm 56: 'Trust in God under persecution'
Psalm 57: 'Prayer for rescue from persecutors'
Psalm 58: 'Prayer for vindication'
Psalm 60: 'Prayer for national victory after defeat'
Psalm 61: 'Assurance of God's eternal protection'
Psalm 64: 'Prayer for protection from secret enemies'
Psalm 70: 'Prayer for quick help'
Psalm 71: 'Prayer for lifelong protection and help'
Psalm 74: 'Prayer for national deliverance from oppressors'
Psalm 77: 'Comfort derived from God's mighty deeds'
Psalm 79: 'Prayer for deliverance from national enemies'
Psalm 80: 'Prayer for Israel's restoration'
Psalm 85: 'Prayer for God's favour'
Psalm 86: 'Prayer for help and guidance'

Psalm 90: 'God's eternity and human frailty'
Psalm 94: 'God the avenger of the righteous'
Psalm 102: 'Prayer to the eternal King for help'
Psalm 108: 'Assurance of God's victory over enemies'
Psalm 120: 'Prayer for deliverance from slanderers'
Psalm 123: 'Prayer for mercy'
Psalm 126: 'A song of ascents'
Psalm 129: 'Prayer for deliverance from enemies'
Psalm 130: 'Waiting for divine redemption'
Psalm 141: 'Prayer for preservation from evil'
Psalm 142: 'Prayer for deliverance from persecutors'
Psalm 143: 'Prayer for deliverance and guidance'

Examples of Psalms for Themes

D1.1 Silence and Presence: Psalm 2
D1.2 Waiting: Psalm 42
D1.3 Darkness: Psalm 25
D1.4 Disorientation: Psalm 27
D1.5 Community and Witness: Psalm 44
D1.6 Memory: Psalm 77
D1.7 Vulnerability: Psalm 6
D1.8 Lament: create your own psalm

Example of a personal psalm of lament

Psalms of Lament are broadly composed of three parts:

1 Address to God
2 Complaint/Lament and Petition
3 Praise

You are invited to include these parts in the creation of your own psalm of lament. You can create as many verses as you like and your psalm is supposed to reflect your own lament. Below is an example of a psalm of lament created after the death of a loved one.

O God, my Heavenly Mother, You are mighty and strong;
You are always here with me when I need You.

O God, my Heavenly Mother, You are loving and kind;
You are always listening when I call upon Your Holy Name.

Why, oh why have You forsaken me, why have You forsaken
my family;
why have You taken my earthly mother too soon to
Your kingdom?

Why is she not here to embrace me, why is she not here
with her smile;
why is she not here with her kind words, why is she not here
with her love?

Do not leave me alone in this darkness, help me to bear
this pain;
give strength to my family and me, be our Beloved here
on Earth.

Help me to understand Your plan, fill that void in my heart;
come and embrace me in my time of need with Your warm
and tender love.

O God, my Heavenly Mother, only You are loving and kind;
I trust in You, O God, for all eternity.

O God, my Heavenly Mother, only You are mighty
and strong;
may Your Holy Name be praised now and forever.

D2: CANTICLES

Below you can find some examples of canticles for use. They are organised by Theme (see pages xxvi–xxvii). If you are in doubt or are not sure which canticle to choose, we recommend the *Nunc Dimittis* (D2.8).

D2.1   Recommended canticle for Silence and Presence

See, the home of God is among mortals.
He will dwell with them;
Death will be no more.

They will be His peoples
and God Himself will be with them;
Death will be no more.

He will wipe every tear from their eyes.
Death will be no more.

Mourning and crying and pain will be no more,
for the first things have passed away.
Death will be no more.

Glory to the Father, and to the Son,
and to the Holy Spirit;
as it was in the beginning, is now
and shall be for ever. Amen.

TRL, p. 118

D2.2   Recommended canticle for Waiting

Jesus, saviour of the world, come to us in Your mercy;
we look to You to save and help us.

By Your cross and Your life laid down, You set Your
    people free:
we look to You to save and help us.

When they were ready to perish, You saved Your disciples:
we look to You to come to our help.

In the greatness of Your mercy, loose us from our chains:
forgive the sins of all Your people.

Make Yourself known as our Saviour and
    Mighty Deliverer:
save and help us, that we may praise You.

Come now, and dwell with us, Lord Christ Jesus:
hear our prayer and be with us always.

And when You come in Your glory, make us to be one
    with You,
and to share the life of Your kingdom.

Glory to the Father …

TRL, 103

D2.3   Recommended canticle for Darkness

Lord almighty and God of our ancestors,
You who made heaven and earth in all their glory.

All things tremble with awe at Your presence,
before Your great and mighty power.

Immeasurable and unsearchable is Your promised mercy,
for You are God, Most High.

You are full of compassion, long-suffering and
    very merciful,
and You relent at human suffering.

O God, according to Your great goodness,
You have promised forgiveness for repentance
to those who have sinned against You.

The sins I have committed against You,
are more in number than the sands of the sea.

I am not worthy to look up to the height of heaven,
because of the multitude of my iniquities.

And now I bend the knee of my heart before You,
imploring Your kindness upon me.

I have sinned, O God, I have sinned,
and I acknowledge my transgressions.

Unworthy as I am, You will save me,
according to Your great mercy.

For all the boast of heaven sings Your praise,
and Your glory is for ever and ever.

Glory to the Father ...

CWDP, 'The Song of Manasseh', p. 240

D2.4   **Recommended canticle for Disorientation**

Seek the Lord while He may be found,
call upon Him while He is near;

Let the wicked abandoned their ways,
and the unrighteousness their thoughts;

Return to the Lord, who will have mercy,
to our God, who will richly pardon.

'For my thoughts are not your thoughts,
neither are my ways your ways', says the Lord.

'For as the heavens are higher than the earth,
so are my ways higher than your ways
and my thoughts than your thoughts.

'As the rain and the snow come down from above,
and return not again but water the earth,

'Bringing forth life and giving growth,
seed for sowing and bread to eat,

'So is the word that goes forth from my mouth;
it will not return to me fruitless,

'But it will accomplish that which I purpose,
and succeed in the task I gave it.'

Glory to the Father ...

CCP, 'A Song of the Word of the Lord',
(drawn from Isaiah 55.6–11), p. 138

D2.5 Recommended canticle for Community and Witness

Jesus, like a mother You gather Your people to You;
You are gentle with us as a mother with her children.

Despair turns to hope through Your sweet goodness;
through Your gentleness we find comfort in fear.

Your warmth gives life to the dead;
Your touch makes sinners righteous.

Lord Jesus, in Your mercy heal us;
in Your love and tenderness remake us.

In Your compassion bring grace and forgiveness,
for the beauty of heaven may Your love prepare us.

Glory to the Father ...

CWDP, 'The Song of Anselm', p. 66

D2.6 Recommended canticle for Memory

Lord Jesus, think on me,
and purge away my sin;
from earth borne passions set me free
and make me pure within.

Lord Jesus, think on me,
with many a care oppressed;
let me Thy loving servant be
and taste Thy promised rest.

Lord Jesus, think on me,
nor let me go astray;
through darkness and perplexity
point Thou the heavenly way.

Lord Jesus, think on me,
that, when the flood is past,
I may the eternal brightness see
and share Thy joy at last.

Glory to the Father ...

CWDP, 'George the Sinner',
tr. A. W. Chatfield, p. 244

D2.7   Recommended canticle for Vulnerability

Christ suffered for you, leaving you an example,
that you should follow in His steps.

He committed no sin, no guile was found on His lips,
when He was reviled, He did not revile in turn.

When He suffered, He did not threaten,
but He trusted Himself to God who judges justly.

Christ Himself bore our sins in His body on the tree,
that we might die to sin and live to righteousness.

By His wounds, you have been healed,
for you were straying like a sheep,
but have now returned
to the shepherd and guardian of your soul.

Glory to the Father ...

CWDP, 'A Song of Christ the Servant'
(drawn from 1 Peter 2.21–25), p. 246

D2.8   Recommended canticle for Lament

Now, Lord, You let Your servant go in peace:
Your word has been fulfilled.

My own eyes have seen the salvation
which You have prepared before the sight of every people;

A light to reveal You to the nations
and the glory of Your people Israel.

Glory to the Father ...

CWDP, 'The *Nunc Dimittis*'
(drawn from Luke 2.29–32)

E: Creeds and Affirmations of Faith

Purpose of the Affirmations

These affirmations are crafted to serve as spiritual tools for reflection and support during Holy Saturday observances. They aim to provide a space for individuals to engage with their current experiences of waiting, silence and presence in a manner that is grounded in Trinitarian theology without rushing to the themes of resurrection and hope. All the Building Blocks offered in this section have been specifically written for the Themes.

Incorporation into Liturgy

Suggestions for incorporating these affirmations into your services include:

- Reading them during moments of silent reflection.
- Using them as part of your prayers of the people – see also Section F.
- Offering them in printed form for personal meditation before or after the service.

By offering these affirmations with the accompanying guidance and considerations, leaders can provide a valuable resource that respects the solemnity of Holy Saturday, acknowledges the complexities of human suffering, and supports the spiritual journey of their congregations with sensitivity and care.

E1: SILENCE AND PRESENCE

E1.1   I believe in the Father, who shapes the silence
of the universe,
in the Son, who walked quietly among us,
and in the Spirit, who whispers truth in moments
of solitude.
This divine silence surrounds me, affirming God's
presence in the quiet.

E1.2   I believe in God the Father, who created the silence
before the world began,
in Jesus Christ, the Son, who endured the silence
of the tomb,
and in the Holy Spirit, who speaks in the
stillness of my heart.
In this divine silence, I am never alone.

E1.3   **Antiphonal option**

Leader: In the silence of creation, who is with us?
People: **God the Father, creator of silence.**
Leader: In the silence of the tomb, who abides with us?
People: **Jesus Christ, who sanctified the silence.**
Leader: In the stillness of our hearts, who speaks?
People: **The Holy Spirit, the whispering Divine Presence.**

E2: WAITING

E2.1   I believe in the Father, who ordains times of waiting,
in the Son, whose life exemplified patience,
and in the Spirit, who nurtures growth in the hidden
depths of our lives.
In this waiting, I am held by a God who values
my remaking.

E2.2   I believe in the Father, who watches over the times
and seasons,
in the Son, who waited in the garden and on the cross,
and in the Spirit, who sustains us in our waiting,
transforming us from glory to glory.

E2.3   **Antiphonal option**

Leader: Who ordains the times and seasons of waiting?
People: **God the Father, keeper of time.**
Leader: Who shared in our deepest waits and sorrows?
People: **Jesus Christ, who waited in obedience.**
Leader: Who renews our strength as we wait?
People: **The Holy Spirit, transforming us from within.**

E3: DARKNESS

E3.1   I believe in the Father, who watches over the night,
in the Son, who was no stranger to darkness,
and in the Spirit, who guides us through the shadows.
This journey through darkness is one I do not walk alone,
for God's presence is constant.

E3.2   I believe in God the Father, who called light
out of darkness,
in Jesus Christ, the Son, who endured the darkness
of death,
and in the Holy Spirit, who guides us through
every shadow,
teaching us that even darkness is not dark to You.

E3.3 Antiphonal option

Leader: In the beginning, who called light from darkness?
People: **God the Father, the initiator of light.**
Leader: In the darkest hour, who was forsaken?
People: **Jesus Christ, the light in our darkness.**
Leader: Through our night, who leads us forth?
People: **The Holy Spirit, illuminating our paths.**

E4: DISORIENTATION

E4.1 I believe in the Father, whose ways are beyond
understanding,
in the Son, who navigated life's complexities,
and in the Spirit, who provides clarity amid confusion.
In my disorientation I find a God who is unfazed
by uncertainty,
offering steadiness as I find my way.

E4.2 I believe in the Father, whose ways are higher than
our ways,
in the Son, who navigated the disorientation of betrayal
and death,
and in the Spirit, who leads us into all truth,
grounding us when the world shifts beneath our feet.

E4.3 Antiphonal option

Leader: When lost and disoriented, who understands
our ways?
People: **God the Father, whose ways are beyond.**
Leader: Who walked the path of utmost disorientation
for us?
People: **Jesus Christ, steadfast through betrayal and
death.**
Leader: Who guides us into truth amid our confusion?
People: **The Holy Spirit, our compass and guide.**

E5: COMMUNITY AND WITNESS

E5.1   I believe in the Father, who gathers us into a
divine family,
in the Son, who shows us the power of community,
and in the Spirit, who knits our hearts together.
In this community, I find a place where shared silence
and mutual presence speak volumes.

E5.2   I believe in the Father, who gathers us as a family,
in Jesus Christ, the Son, who shows us the power of
community through His life and sacrifice,
and in the Holy Spirit, who binds us together in love,
bearing witness to the truth that in our shared suffering,
we may find shared strength.

E5.3   **Antiphonal option**

Leader: Who calls us into divine family and community?
People: **God the Father, the architect of fellowship.**
Leader: Whose life exemplifies the power of communal
witness?
People: **Jesus Christ, who unites us in His sacrifice.**
Leader: Who knits our hearts together in love?
People: **The Holy Spirit, weaving us into one.**

E6: MEMORY

E6.1   I believe in the Father, who remembers each moment
of creation,
the Son, whose life on earth reveals divine love to us,
and in the Spirit, who helps us to recall the presence of
God in all things.
My memories, held within God's grace, remind me of a
presence that transcends time.

E6.2   I believe in God the Father, who remembers His
covenant forever,
in Jesus Christ, the Son, whose acts of love and sacrifice
are etched into the fabric of history,
and in the Holy Spirit, who helps us to recall all that
God has spoken to us,
teaching us to find meaning in our memories, held
within the sacred heart of God.

E6.3   **Antiphonal option**

Leader: Who remembers His covenant across the ages?
People: **God the Father, eternal in remembrance.**
Leader: Whose life and death are forever remembered
for our sake?
People: **Jesus Christ, whose love is our eternal memory.**
Leader: Who stirs in us the memory of divine words
and deeds?
People: **The Holy Spirit, our reminder and revealer.**

E7: VULNERABILITY

E7.1   I believe in the Father, who embraces our humanity,
in the Son, who lived a life of openness,
and in the Spirit, who empowers us in our authenticity.
In my vulnerability I am not weak but deeply connected
to the Divine,
a testament to the strength found in genuine being.

E7.2   I believe in the Father, who created us in His image,
embracing our fragility,
in Jesus Christ, the Son, who in vulnerability bore our
sins and sorrows,
and in the Holy Spirit, who comforts us in our suffering,
showing us that in our most vulnerable moments, we
are not forsaken but deeply known and loved.

E7.3 Antiphonal option

Leader: In our vulnerability, who sees us and loves us still?
People: **God the Father, who crafted our hearts.**
Leader: Who embraced vulnerability to the point of
death for us?
People: **Jesus Christ, our strength in weakness.**
Leader: Who brings comfort to our vulnerable spirits?
People: **The Holy Spirit, our advocate and comforter.**

E8: LAMENT

E8.1 I believe in the Father, who hears our deepest concerns,
in the Son, who empathises with human sorrow,
and in the Spirit, who intercedes on our behalf.
My lament is a sacred conversation with the Divine,
where I am heard and held in the vastness of God's
understanding.

E8.2 I believe in the Father, who hears our cries,
in Jesus Christ, the Son, who laments over Jerusalem and
cried out in forsakenness,
and in the Holy Spirit, who intercedes for us with groans
too deep for words.
In my lament, I am joined to the suffering of Christ,
finding in my cries a sacred echo of His own,
a lament that is held and honoured by the Trinity,
assuring me that in my deepest pain,
I am not alone, but deeply connected to the heart of God.

E8.3 Antiphonal option

Leader: When we cry out in our pain, who hears us?
People: **God the Father, who listens to every cry.**
Leader: Who shares in the depths of human lament?
People: **Jesus Christ, who knows our suffering.**
Leader: Who intercedes for us in our silent grief?
People: **The Holy Spirit, who voices our wordless prayers.**

F: Prayers and Movement

Prayer is an essential part of any service/church space. It can be traced back to the Scriptures, where different characters pronounce prayers of praise and thanksgiving, raise their petitions and lament in times of difficulty, and it is widely practised by Christians around the world to communicate with the Triune God. This section contains collects, Stations of the Sacred Pause, intercessions and invitations to the Lord's Prayer. Some movement during the prayers is suggested but is optional. It is up to the leader to make sure the congregation knows that movement is not a requirement, and up to the people to do what is most comfortable for them.

Collects

Collects are prayers that are meant to gather the intentions of the people and the focus of worship into a concise form. There are three collects offered, all exploring the Themes of this resource. The last collect is an example of a 'breath prayer' that is based on the prayers of Cole Arthur Riley.[1] Riley defines this type of prayer as an ancient practice of connecting deep breathing with short, memorable phrases. Breath prayers allow the grounding of one's body in space, and connect the body, mind and soul together. Breath prayers might be also used in an intercessory form.

Movement: there is no specific movement for the collect. Usually, the congregation stays seated.

Stations of the Sacred Pause

There are two sets of the stations offered. The first set has the traditional number of 14 stations of the cross and is cross-oriented. It might be helpful for those people who find comfort in focusing on the cross and the redemptive work of Jesus on the cross. However, it might not be suitable for all and it is up to the leader/minister to decide whether this set will be suitable for their congregation.

This first set combines stations that are traditionally used in churches with some newly created stations. The traditional stations (Sections F2.1.1 – F2.1.11) cover a period from Gethsemane to the tomb, remembering the events of Good Friday and the time when Jesus was physically alive. The last three sections (F2.1.12 – F2.1.14) are created specifically for this resource to give space to reflect on what was happening between the events of Good Friday and Easter Sunday. They are focused on the actions of Jesus, the Holy Spirit and the disciples, actions which are not mentioned in the Gospels. They are offered as an imaginative exercise to help people to place themselves in the liminal space of Holy Saturday, the space which might be inhabited at any stage of one's spiritual life. Sections F2.1.12 and F2.1.13 are based on Shelly Rambo's ideas of the nature of Jesus' descent to Hell and on the actions of the Holy Spirit in the world after Jesus dies on the cross. According to Rambo, Jesus descends to Hell not victoriously, as it is quite often pictured in the Church tradition (i.e. 'harrowing of Hell'), but quietly. It is that quiet presence that makes a difference for people who exist in that liminal space.[2] The Themes of presence and witness also have a prominent place in the life of a trauma survivor, where being quietly present and witnessing to one's pain can mean more than attempts to 'fix' things.

The Holy Spirit of Holy Saturday occupies an important place in Rambo's theology. She reflects on what happens within the Holy Trinity after Jesus dies. The Father and the Son are at the farthest ends from each other (Jesus feels the Father's absence before He dies), and after the Son dies, He descends to Hell and stays there until His resurrection. Consequently, both the Father and the Son are unavailable in this liminal period of grieving and pain. This leaves us with the Holy Spirit, who was breathed into the world when Jesus 'breathed His last' (Matt. 27.50; Mark 15.37; Luke 23.46). It is the Holy Spirit that becomes a witness between Good Friday and Easter Sunday, seeing the pain and confusion of the disciples and being present in their disorientation and grief.[3]

The second set of stations is non cross-oriented and is newly created for this resource. Rather than following the traditional pattern of remembering the Passion of Jesus, this set focuses on the Themes offered in this book to form their own Stations of the Sacred Pause. These might suit better those who do not necessarily want to focus on the violence of the cross and do not see the cross as a place of comfort.

Movement: the stations are not created to be used exclusively during the service. They can be used either during the service wherever people feel comfortable to do so, or outside of the service as a separate prayerful space. At each station there should be a short summary of what the station represents and a prayer that people might use. The stations might be a creative space where art in different forms is represented, and it is up to the leader to decide how to organise them. Prayer movements might also be organised differently depending on the station. For example, at the memory station, people might be encouraged to write down their prayers/petitions and put them on a 'prayer tree'. The number of stations might be reduced depending on the size of the church space.

Intercessions

Intercessions are corporate prayers for the needs of the Church and the world. More intercessions might be created if needed.

Movement: people might be sitting or kneeling for the intercessions. Some additional movement might be offered depending on the Theme explored. A prayer tree may also be used in this section as well as other forms of embodied prayer. For example, when intercessions of vulnerability are being used, people might write down their prayers/concerns on stones and bring them to the altar.

Invitation to the Lord's Prayer

The Lord's Prayer is the most famous prayer that comes from Jesus Himself and it is an essential part of Christian worship. There are three invitations offered, two coming from *New Patterns of Worship* and one created for this resource, and two variations of the Lord's Prayer.

Movement: people might want to stay seated or to kneel.

F1: COLLECTS

F1.1   Almighty God, we find ourselves in a sacred pause,
        we hold space for our grief, our uncertainties, and the
            deep yearnings of our hearts.
        Grant us, O Lord, the grace to dwell here with faith
            and patience.
        Teach us to listen for Your still, small voice in the midst
            of our waiting,
        reminding us that even in the darkest night,
        Your love and presence are unwavering.

        Comfort all who carry the weight of trauma and loss,
        enveloping them in Your peace that surpasses
            understanding.
        Strengthen our community, that we may offer solace
            and support to one another
        as we journey through the shadows.

        As we reflect on the mystery of Your love, help us to feel
            Your grace.

May this time draw us closer to You and to each other,
forging bonds of compassion and understanding.

We ask this in the name of Jesus Christ, as we wait in
the silence of the tomb.

Amen.

F1.2 Lord God, on this day of waiting and listening,
we gather to remember the life and death of Your Son,
Jesus Christ.

We come to You as a community to witness to the great
mystery of our faith,
keeping in mind those who cannot be here today
because of the oppression and injustice that they
have experienced
and because of the wounds and the scars that they bear
as a result.

We come to You in mourning for the darkness we see in
the world,
and the struggles that so many people endure.

We acknowledge our vulnerability, knowing that
Your Son
experienced it as we are, even to the point of death.

We come to pause and think about the space that
we hold
as the disciples did after Jesus died and before the hope
had been revealed.

We come to this sacred space to be quietly present, to
share our struggles,
to lament about the state of the world and to be
witnesses to each other's experiences.

We pray in Your name, remembering Your Son and
asking for the Holy Spirit to come in the midst of us.

Amen.

F1.3 Breath collect

Lord God, we come to You today to remember
both the life and death of Your Son,
and the lives and experiences of the disciples.
We come to be in a space where nothing is certain,
where quiet prayers are being offered, and silent
    presence is lived out.

Inhale: We come together and breathe in,
Exhale: acknowledging our bodily presence in this space.

We come in solidarity with the disciples,
knowing how difficult it was for them to accept
the death of their beloved teacher and friend;
how shocked they were, how deep their grief was,
and how strong was their sense of disorientation.

Inhale: We come together and breathe in,
Exhale: acknowledging our shared humanity and
    vulnerability in this space.

We come to You bringing our own fears, questions
    and doubts,
we come uncertain, we come quietly, we come grieving
    and lost.
We bring all of ourselves: our bodies, our minds, our
    spirits and our souls,
we come to be together to reflect on where God is and
    where we are
in the space of the sacred pause.

Inhale: We come together and breathe in,
Exhale: knowing that all feelings are valid in this space.

We come in the name of the Father, the Son
    and the Holy Spirit.

Amen.

F2: STATIONS OF THE SACRED PAUSE

These prayers may be used for different stations set up around the church – each prayer to be read at a new station. The traditional number of stations (14) is provided, but this can be changed due to limitations of space, time or suitability for your context. Each prayer relates to particular Themes, named in brackets, which could be explored further at each station.

F2.1 Cross-oriented stations

F2.1.1 Jesus in agony in Gethsemane (Darkness, Vulnerability)

Lord Jesus, You entered the garden of fear
and faced the agony of Your impending death:
be with those who share that agony
and face death unwillingly this day.
You shared our fear and knew the weakness of
   our humanity:
give strength and hope to the dispirited and despairing.
To You, Jesus, who sweated blood,
be honour and glory with the Father and the Holy Spirit,
now and for ever.
Amen.

CWTS, 'The Way of the Cross'

F2.1.2 Jesus betrayed and arrested (Darkness, Vulnerability)

Lord Jesus, You were betrayed by the kiss of a friend:
be with those who are betrayed and slandered and
   falsely accused.
You knew the experience of having Your love
thrown back in Your face for mere silver:
be with families which are torn apart by mistrust
   or temptation.
To You, Jesus, who offered Your face to Your betrayer,
be honour and glory with the Father and the Holy Spirit,
now and for ever. **Amen.**

CWTS, 'The Way of the Cross'

F2.1.3   Jesus condemned by the Sanhedrin (Darkness, Lament)

Lord Jesus, You were the victim of religious bigotry:
be with those who are persecuted by small-minded
    authority.
You faced the condemnation of fearful hearts:
deepen the understanding of those who shut themselves
    off from the experience and wisdom of others.
To You, Jesus, unjustly judged victim,
be honour and glory with the Father and the Holy Spirit,
now and for ever.
Amen.

CWTS, 'The Way of the Cross'

F2.1.4   Peter denies Jesus (Darkness, Disorientation, Lament)

Lord Jesus, as Peter betrayed You,
You experienced the double agony of love rejected and
    friendship denied:
be with those who know no friends and are rejected
    by society.
You understood the fear within Peter:
help us to understand the anxieties of those who fear
    for their future.
To You, Jesus, who gazed with sadness at Your
    lost friend,
be honour and glory with the Father and the Holy Spirit,
now and for ever.
Amen.

CWTS, 'The Way of the Cross'

F2.1.5   Jesus judged by Pilate
(Darkness, Vulnerability, Witness)

Lord Jesus, You were condemned to death for political
    expediency:
be with those who are imprisoned for the convenience
    of the powerful.

You were the victim of unbridled injustice:
change the minds and motivations of oppressors and
    exploiters to Your way of peace.
To You, Jesus, innocent though condemned,
be honour and glory with the Father and the Holy Spirit,
now and for ever.
Amen.

CWTS, 'The Way of the Cross'

**F2.1.6 Jesus scourged and crowned with thorns
(Vulnerability, Witness, Memory)**

Lord Jesus, You faced the torment of barbaric
    punishment and mocking tongue:
be with those who cry out in physical agony and
    emotional distress.
You endured unbearable abuse:
be with those who face torture and mockery in our
    world today.
To You, Jesus, the King crowned with thorns,
be honour and glory with the Father and the Holy Spirit,
now and for ever.
Amen.

CWTS, 'The Way of the Cross'

**F2.1.7 Jesus carries the cross
(Darkness, Witness, Vulnerability)**

Lord Jesus, You carried the cross through the rough
    streets of Jerusalem:
be with those who are loaded with the burdens beyond
    their strength.
You bore the weight of our sins when You carried
    the cross:
help us to realise the extent and the cost of Your
    love for us.

To You, Jesus, bearing a cross not Your own,
be honour and glory with the Father and the Holy Spirit,
now and for ever.
Amen.

CWTS, 'The Way of the Cross'

F2.1.8 Jesus is crucified (Disorientation, Witness)

Lord Jesus, You bled in pain as the nails were driven
    into Your flesh:
transform through the mystery of Your love the pain of
    those who suffer.
To You, Jesus, our crucified Lord,
be honour and glory with the Father and the Holy Spirit,
now and for ever.
Amen.

CWTS, 'The Way of the Cross'

F2.1.9 Jesus on the cross; His mother and His friend (Darkness, Community)

Lord Jesus, Your mother and Your dearest friend
    stayed with You to the bitter end,
yet even while racked with pain You ministered to them:
be with all broken families today
and care for those who long for companionship.
You cared for Your loved ones even in Your death-throes:
give us a love for one another
that is stronger even than the fear of death.
To you, Jesus, loving in the face of death,
be honour and glory with the Father and the Holy Spirit,
now and for ever.
Amen.

CWTS, 'The Way of the Cross'

F2.1.10 Jesus dies on the cross (Darkness, Lament, Witness)

Lord Jesus, You died on the cross
and entered the bleakest of all circumstances:
give courage to those who die at the hands of others.
In death You entered the darkest place of all:
illumine our darkness with Your glorious presence.
To You, Jesus, Your lifeless body hanging on the tree
    of shame,
be honour and glory with the Father and the Holy Spirit,
now and for ever.
Amen.

CWTS, 'The Way of the Cross'

F2.1.11 Jesus laid in the tomb (Darkness, Waiting, Community)

Lord Jesus, Lord of life, You became as nothing for us:
be with those who feel worthless and as nothing in the
    world's eyes.
You were laid in a cold, dark tomb and hidden
    from sight:
be with all who suffer and die in secret,
hidden from the eyes of the world.
To You, Jesus, Your rigid body imprisoned in a tomb,
be honour and glory with the Father and the Holy Spirit,
now and for ever.
Amen.

CWTS, 'The Way of the Cross'

F2.1.12 Jesus descends to Hell (Darkness, Waiting, Witness)

Lord Jesus, as You breathed Your last on the cross,
You went to Hell to be with those who were waiting in
    darkness and silence.
It was not Your victorious appearance that liberated
    them but Your quiet presence,
Your acknowledgement of their pain and Your solidarity
with those for whom there seemed to be no way out.

Through being with them and witnessing to
    their suffering,
You showed Your love and compassion;
it was that presence and that love that made
    a difference.
To You, Jesus, present when You are needed most,
be honour and glory with the Father and the Holy Spirit.
Amen.

F2.1.13 The Holy Spirit as the witness
(Waiting, Witness, Community)

Holy Spirit, You revealed yourself in the world when
    the Son of God breathed His last.
You were in the world when the Father was mourning
    His Son,
and when the Son was quietly present in Hell with
    children of the Most High.
You witnessed the disciples being devastated after the
    loss of their beloved teacher and friend,
You saw the tears and lament of Mary and the other
    women who followed Jesus to the cross,
You felt how lost and hopeless Jesus' followers were
    and You were there to comfort them.
In this period of darkness, disorientation and lament,
You were there with each breath that humanity
    was taking.
To You, Holy Spirit, who presented Yourself in the
    time of utmost need,
to You, the Comforter in darkest times,
be honour and glory with the Father and the Son,
now and for ever.
Amen.

F2.1.14 The disciples mourn the loss of Jesus (Disorientation, Lament, Community)

With the disciples who were shocked by the death of
    their teacher and friend,
with the disciples who felt abandoned and lost, who
    could not think straight because of their grief,
with the disciples who were in pain and could not make
    sense of what had happened,
we gather today to be together in this time, to share our
    sorrows and pain,
to witness to the end of Jesus' life, to Him going to Hell
    to be with the silenced and forgotten,
to see the Comforter who witnesses the pain of the
    world in the most difficult times.
We as the disciples of the contemporary time, as a
community of witnesses, remember the pain and
suffering of Jesus, the Father's grief and the Holy
Spirit's witness of the world covered in darkness.
We give honour and glory to the Holy Trinity,
now and for ever.
Amen.

F2.2 Non cross-oriented stations

F2.2.1 Silence and Presence

We come quietly, we come silently,
to be present, to be aware,
to hold the sacred space,
to pause and to reflect on the life and death of
    Jesus Christ,
and on our lives where there might be too much silence
or not nearly enough,
where we live our lives without being present
or where we are so aware of what is going on
that it makes our lives almost unbearable.
We come to the sacred space to reflect on silence and
    presence together.

We come in the name of the Father, the Son,
and the Holy Spirit.
Amen.

F2.2.2 Waiting

We come to wait and to be transformed through
this waiting,
knowing that transformation is different for everyone;
staying away from judgement and offering to support
one another.
Waiting might be tiring and uncertain, and
transformation might be difficult to imagine.
We come together as our lives are intertwined;
we pray that in the waiting with others we might
find strength.
We come to the sacred space to reflect on waiting and
transforming together.
We come in the name of the Father, the Son,
and the Holy Spirit.
Amen.

F2.2.3 Darkness

We come knowing that there is so much darkness
around us,
acknowledging that sometimes we might feel like there
is no hope.
We remember Jesus praying in the darkness
in Gethsemane,
and how the darkness covered the world when Jesus
breathed His last.
We know that darkness will always be in the world
but we are looking at the darkness of the tomb,
knowing that not all darkness stays in the world.
We wait at the tomb while Jesus is quietly present in Hell
with all those from the creation of the world
to the day when the Son of God had died.

We come to the sacred space to reflect on
  darkness together.
We come in the name of the Father, the Son,
  and the Holy Spirit.
Amen.

F2.2.4 Disorientation

We come to remember how frightened the disciples
  were when Jesus was arrested
and how they abandoned Him and were dispersed.
We remember how lost they felt and how they could
  not make sense of what had happened.
We acknowledge that quite often we experience the
  same sense of disorientation,
how confused and puzzled we are when something
  unexpected and challenging happens.
We come bringing our own confusion and questions,
  fear and doubts.
We come to the sacred space to reflect on
  disorientation together.
We come in the name of the Father, the Son,
  and the Holy Spirit.
Amen.

F2.2.5 Community and Witness

We come to share our own experiences with each other,
knowing how powerful it might be to be around others,
and to support each other in whatever is happening in
  our lives.
Today we come to share our pain over the death of Jesus,
but also to share our pain over the loss of those whom
  we love,
the pain of separation, the pain of irreconcilable
  differences,

the pain of division and alienation in families and
	friendships.
We come knowing that each of us has been through
	this pain
and that we can support each other through love and
	compassion.
We come to the sacred space to reflect on what it means
	to be a community.
We come in the name of the Father, the Son,
	and the Holy Spirit.
Amen.

F2.2.6 Memory

We come to acknowledge that we all have things we
	want to remember,
and things we would like to forget,
and the things that keep coming back even when we do
	not want them to.
We know how complicated memory can be
and how difficult it might be to remember.
Today we remember all the years of Jesus'
	earthly ministry
and His journey towards His death.
We know that even though it might be challenging
to think about His pain and the end of His life,
we can do it together as a community
and support each other in our remembrance.
We come to the sacred space to reflect on
	memory together.
We come in the name of the Father, the Son,
	and the Holy Spirit.
Amen.

F2.2.7 Vulnerability

We come to acknowledge our vulnerability as part of
 our human life,
and to remember that it is normal to be vulnerable, not
 something to be ashamed of.
We know that God became vulnerable for our sake
and experienced vulnerability to the end of Christ's
 earthly life.
As we gather today, we are here to support each other
and to be together as a community of vulnerable
 human beings.
We come to the sacred space to reflect on
 vulnerability together.
We come in the name of the Father, the Son,
 and the Holy Spirit.
Amen.

F2.2.8 Lament

We come to lament over the world we live in,
over the injustice, oppression and neglect,
over indifference, egoism and the lack of support.
We know that all of this was present when Jesus
 walked the earth,
and that He was always compassionate and loving
 towards humanity.
We lament, but we also want to follow His example
of the kindness, mercy, and care that He extended to
 everyone that needed it.
We come to the sacred space to lament together.
We come in the name of the Father, the Son,
 and the Holy Spirit.
Amen.

F3: INTERCESSIONS

F3.1   Silence and Presence

Lord God, we are here today to leave our prayers
with You in the stillness and quietness of the moment
without rush, impatience or the noise of big words.
We come together knowing that sometimes we find
ourselves in this place without time, where the words
not spoken and the feelings not shown need to find a
space to exist and to be acknowledged more than we
ever know.

We come to You to be present together, to listen to our
hearts and minds, and to share silence together.

Pause

For the world that is busy, restless, and so often
ignorant of the struggles and needs of Your creation.
We dwell in silence.

Pause

For those who are invisible to power structures and are
neglected by society, for the unhoused, the imprisoned,
for refugees, orphans and all those without support.
We dwell in silence.

Pause

For those who struggle because society has never been
built for them, for neurodivergent people, those with
disabilities, for all those who are unheard and whose
needs are not met.
We dwell in silence.

Pause

For all those who stay silent against their will, for those in unsafe environments, for those who are not free to live authentically. For those who live with depression and anxiety, and for those who do not see a reason to wake up in the morning.
We dwell in silence.

Pause

For those who stay silent because they are not able to put into words what they are going through, for those who do not have support structures in place, for those who have lost trust in people and institutions, and for those that we see every day without ever noticing their struggles.
We dwell in silence.

Pause

For those who are just finding their way in the world, who are learning how to speak up and protect their boundaries, learning how to build healthy relationships, and learning to be in harmony with themselves, and for all those who are not there yet.
We dwell in silence.

Pause

Lord, in this moment we bring to You everything that we have in our hearts, things that we might be struggling with and things that we might not be ready to share with anyone yet. Be present with us in our silent prayer and help us to acknowledge and appreciate each other in this sacred space.

A moment of silence to bring your own prayers and petitions to God

F3.2 Waiting

In this moment of waiting and longing we come to God, knowing that we all find ourselves waiting for something in our lives. We acknowledge the reality of waiting and we stand in solidarity with others who exist in this liminal space.

Pause

With those who are unsafe and live from day to day without any certainty of what comes next, we long for safety, protection, stability and peace.
With them we wait and pray.

With those who have been wronged, who cry for justice but who have not been able to see it being served, with all who have been divided by disagreements and have not been able to find a way forward, we long for justice and reconciliation.
With them we wait and pray.

With those who have been let down by their families, institutions, society and the Church, with the invisible, forgotten, marginalised, we long for love, support and a sense of belonging.
With them we wait and pray.

With those who are going through difficult times, who are fighting battles no one knows about, with those who feel like they cannot cope with life anymore, we long for strength, acknowledgement and support.
With them we wait and pray.

With those who are lonely, isolated, misunderstood, with those who want to change their lives but who are afraid to start their journey, we long for relationships, community and the bravery to step out of the comfort of what is known and start anew.
With them we wait and pray.

Lord God, we all know how it feels to wait for something and how difficult it might be to stay in this place of waiting.

Help us to be patient, attentive and understanding towards others whom we might meet on the journey. Help us to see if we can support someone to make their waiting easier or shorter or if we can support them through just being present with them. We pray in the name of Your son Jesus Christ, who experienced waiting in His earthly life. **Amen.**

F3.3   Darkness

Lord God, as Your Son Jesus experienced darkness in His earthly life, we too find ourselves in spiritual and physical darkness. It might be hard for us to be in that place, but at the same time darkness might be helpful. It can create a feeling of intimacy, safety and even growth. Holding in mind this complexity, we pray to You in this sacred space.

Pause

As Your Son prayed in Gethsemane, feeling confused, lost and exhausted, we too pray, trying to hold many emotions together, wanting to find peace and clarity. It is not an easy place to be in, but we acknowledge that this experience might bring us closer to You as it happened with Your Son under the olive trees of Gethsemane.
In the darkness, bring us closer to You.

As Your Son felt abandoned on the cross and died when darkness was unfolding on Your whole creation, we think about all times when we have not felt Your presence, when we have felt that You were as far away as possible and that we were left alone. As those moments can indeed be dark, we want to remember that You never truly leave us and that the Holy Spirit witnesses to our struggles and is there to comfort us. **In the darkness, send Your Holy Spirit to comfort us.**

As Your Son was buried in a dark tomb without any light or life, we bring to You all the times when we have felt buried under the weight of our life circumstances, where there is no movement, light or life. As difficult as it might be, we want to acknowledge that the tomb can be a safe space for us to wait, rest and gather our strength before we continue with our journey. As a mother's womb, it can surround us to protect us and to provide us with everything we need on our journey to a new life.
In the darkness, give us rest and strength to move further in our journey.

As the disciples fled under the cover of darkness and were scattered around Jerusalem, we think about all the times when we have been scared, when we have been grieving, when we have lost touch with each other and have been alienated in our struggles. We remember that You sent the Comforter to witness the disciples' pain, fear, and confusion, and that with His/Her[4] help they were able to find each other again and to live through their experience together.
In the darkness, help us to find each other again and to be a community of witness.

Merciful God, in the darkness of our bodies, hearts and minds help us to find intimacy, safety, rest and community, acknowledging that darkness is never only one thing and that in it new things can be born. **Amen.**

F3.4   Disorientation

Lord God, as we travel through life, being on a pilgrimage to Your Holy Kingdom, we all experience confusion and disorientation. Sometimes the path is unclear, and we do not know what our next step should be. When it happens, we do not always come to You straight away. It might take time to orient ourselves towards You again, but we are here today bringing to You what is on our hearts.

Pause

When we are lost and cannot see the road ahead, when we are troubled in body, mind and spirit, when we feel anxious and irritated, when we are overwhelmed to the point that we cannot make any decisions at all, we come to You asking for help and guidance.
In our disorientation, come and be with us.

When we are burdened with difficult experiences, when we feel like our life is falling apart, when things do not go as planned, when nothing is certain, we come to You asking for clarity and strength.
In our disorientation, come and be with us.

When we are confused about who we are or what we want, when we do not know what our calling in life is, when we do not know our own strengths and limitations, we come to You asking for courage to explore what it means to be ourselves.
In our disorientation, come and be with us.

When we are disoriented and confused, it might feel like everything in our lives is chaotic and nothing good can come out of it. Refresh in our minds the account of the world's creation. When we read about it, it might feel chaotic and a bit uncertain, while in fact there is order and beauty in that chaos. Help us to remember that

chaos is not always bad and that great things can be born out of it.
In our disorientation, come and be with us.

When we meet others who are confused and disoriented, when we notice that someone is struggling because of uncertainty in their life, help us to not look away but to step into a space where, with Your guidance, we can be present with each other in support of, and in witness to, each other's disorientation.
In our disorientation, come and be with us.

Merciful God, in our disorientation be with us and accept our prayers for the sake of Your Son, our Saviour Jesus Christ. **Amen.**

F3.5   Community and Witness

We come as a community today to be together in our prayers and witness, to hold this sacred space, to be comforted by each other and by the Holy Spirit, who remains and dwells in this space as the Witness and the Comforter.

Pause

Holy Spirit, as You come among us to remain with us, we thank You for being with us in difficult times. We pray for all those who might not feel Your presence, for all who are isolated, abandoned and forgotten and for those who are lonely and lost. Help them to feel Your presence and to know that they are not alone, and help us to notice those in need of our presence. Encourage us to be present with them as You are present with us.
Holy Spirit, come and remain with us.

Holy Spirit, as You become a witness to our struggles, our pain and grief, our feelings of being lost, unwanted, forgotten, to our heightened sense of justice, especially

when we know that it is not being served, we thank You for the ability to share with You deep thoughts and inclinations of our hearts, to tell our story in a space with no judgement, avoidance or attempts to fix us. As You become our witness, help us to be witnesses to the lives of others, to be good listeners and to create safe spaces where stories can be told.
Holy Spirit, come and witness to our lives.

Holy Spirit, the Comforter, we thank You for coming and comforting us in the midst of struggle. You comfort us when we cry, when we feel angry, when we grieve, when we do not even know what is happening to us. You comfort us when we cannot express what we are going through, when we struggle in silence. Help us to be that comforting presence to others, to create a sense of trust and safety in our community and to help each other in our struggles, building strong relationships in the process.
Holy Spirit, come and comfort us.

Holy Spirit, You are the Spirit of Love that comes and remains with us, witnessing to God's love towards us and to God's wish for us to love each other. As You love us and as You encourage us to love others, be to us a constant reminder that God's love remains in the world and that we who are created in God's image should live in love with our neighbours, who are equally created in God's image.
Holy Spirit, come and teach us to love.

Holy Spirit, we thank You for Your presence and witness, for Your encouragement to love and for Your comfort in our most difficult experiences. To You, along with the Father and the Son, be honour and glory forever.
Amen.

F3.6 Memory

As a community of witnesses, we gather to remember
the life and death of Jesus Christ.

Pause

His love towards each person that He encountered,
We remember.

His solidarity with those who are oppressed and in pain,
We remember.

His sense of justice for those who have been wronged,
We remember.

His presence among those who are in the midst of struggle,
We remember.

His compassion towards those who are excluded and
    forgotten by society,
We remember.

His thoughtfulness and attention to those who
    need support,
We remember.

His gift of forgiveness to those who open their hearts
    to him,
We remember.

As we share our witness,
as we mourn together,
as we pause together to reflect on the life and ministry
    of Jesus,
we bring our prayers and thoughts to the Father who,
    with the Son and the Holy Spirit,
reigns for ever and ever.
Amen.

F3.7   Vulnerability

Lord God, we come to You in a time of vulnerability,
acknowledging how fragile human life is,
remembering that Your Son, Jesus Christ, became fragile
and vulnerable and experienced grief, loss, exhaustion,
pain and death, in solidarity with Your creation.

Pause

In the face of war, disunity and hate,
We come to You with burdened hearts.

In the face of sickness, death and loss,
We come to You with burdened hearts.

In the face of physical, emotional and spiritual struggle,
We come to You with burdened hearts.

In the face of injustice, oppression and neglect,
We come to You with burdened hearts.

In the face of danger to our life, loss of safety and comfort,
We come to You with burdened hearts.

In the face of betrayal, abandonment and
    broken promises,
We come to You with burdened hearts.

In the face of loneliness, isolation and lostness,
We come to You with burdened hearts.

In the face of battles that no one knows we are fighting,
We come to You with burdened hearts.

Merciful Father, we come to You as vulnerable
    as we are,
remembering that Your Son knows all of our sorrows
    and challenges through His own experience.
We ask You to accept our prayers for the sake of Your
    Son, our Saviour, Jesus Christ.
Amen.

F3.8 Lament

We bring our sorrows, our struggles, our doubts into
the presence of God and of each other on the day when
the whole creation pauses to mourn the death of the
Saviour of the world.

Pause

Over the dignity of creation that has been neglected,
used, hurt and side-lined,
We lament.

Over the peace lost, restoration that is not yet present,
and reconciliation that is still far away,
We lament.

Over human indifference, greed, and a deep sense
of injustice,
We lament.

Over human promises not being fulfilled, trust broken,
hope abandoned,
We lament.

Over those who have been hurt, silenced, not believed,
We lament.

Over those who have been powerless and trapped in
their circumstances,
We lament.

Over those who have been wounded by society and by
the Church,
We lament.

Over those who have lost faith and lost hope,
We lament.

We bring our sorrows, our struggles, our doubts into
the presence of God and of each other on the day when

the whole creation pauses to mourn the death of the
Saviour of the world.

Merciful Father, accept our lamentations,
for the sake of Your Son, our Saviour, Jesus Christ.
Amen.

F4: INTRODUCTIONS TO THE LORD'S PRAYER

F4.1   As God's children, and heirs with Christ
we cry in the Spirit, 'Abba', Father.

NPW, F37

F4.2   Lord, remember us in Your kingdom,
as we pray in the words You gave us.

NPW, F38

F4.3   [For use on Holy Saturday]
As we stand at the tomb after the events of the cross,
let us pray as our Saviour has taught us:

**Our Father in heaven,
hallowed be Your name,
Your kingdom come,
Your will be done,
on earth as in heaven.
Give us today our daily bread.
Forgive us our sins as we forgive those
who sin against us.
Lead us not into temptation,
but deliver us from evil.
For the kingdom, the power,
and the glory are Yours
now and for ever.
Amen.**

or

Our Father, who art in heaven,
hallowed be Thy name;
Thy kingdom come;
Thy will be done;
on earth as it is in heaven.
Give us this day our daily bread.
And forgive us our trespasses,
as we forgive those who trespass against us.
And lead us not into temptation;
but deliver us from evil.
For Thine is the kingdom,
the power and the glory
for ever and ever.
Amen.

Notes

1 Cole Arthur Riley, 2024, *Black Liturgies*, Toronto: Penguin Random House, p. xxii.

2 To learn more, read Shelly Rambo, *Spirit and Trauma: A Theology of Remaining*, Louisville, KY: Westminster John Knox Press, ch. 2.

3 To learn more, read Rambo, *Spirit and Trauma*, ch. 4.

4 While the Holy Spirit is traditionally referred to as 'He' in the New Testament and mainstream theology, some theologies use the feminine language of 'She' that is also used in the Hebrew Bible, and it is up to the minister to choose which pronouns to use.

G: Praise and Thanksgiving

The Themes in this resource are derived from that unique time and space of Holy Saturday but are provided for use throughout the year. The Building Blocks provided here are crafted to help your congregation engage deeply with those Themes, offering a balanced approach to worship that acknowledges the solemnity of the day while fostering a reflective atmosphere of reverence and gratitude. For each Theme, incorporating praise and thanksgiving (and songs/hymns found in the last part of this section) can help balance the reflective nature of the observances with expressions of reverence and gratitude towards God's enduring presence and the mysteries of faith.

Here are some suggestions:

G1: Silence and Presence

Thanksgiving: For God's unspoken words that comfort us beyond measure and for His presence in our deepest solitude.
Praise Response: **In the silence, You are God.**

Alternative:
In the quiet of our hearts, we acknowledge Your presence, O God.
We give thanks for Your silent companionship that sustains us.

G2: Waiting

Thanksgiving: For the divine work accomplished in the hiddenness of waiting, shaping our hearts in unseen ways.
Praise Response: **In our waiting, Your love enfolds us.**

Alternative:
In the waiting, we are transformed by Your hand, O Lord.
We praise You for the work You do within us, unseen yet profound.

G3: Darkness

Thanksgiving: For God's guidance through our darkest nights and the promise that darkness is as light to Him.
Praise Response: **Even in darkness, Your light guides us.**

G4: Disorientation

Thanksgiving: For God's patient guidance when we are lost, and for the Spirit's gentle nudge towards reorientation.
Praise Response: **In our wandering, You lead us home.**

Alternative:
When paths twist and turn, You are our constant, O Lord.
For Your steady hand, we offer our praise.

G5: Community and Witness

Thanksgiving: For the gift of community, where shared burdens become lighter, and for the strength found in fellowship.
Praise Response: **Together in Your love, we stand strong.**

Alternative:
In fellowship, we witness Your love, O God.
We give thanks for the community that reflects Your heart.

G6: Memory

Thanksgiving: For God's actions throughout history that remind us of His unchanging faithfulness and love.
Praise Response: **Through our memories, Your faithfulness shines.**

G7: Vulnerability

Thanksgiving: For God's embrace in our most vulnerable moments and for His strength made perfect in our weakness.
Praise Response: **In our openness, Your strength envelops us.**

Alternative:
In our openness before You, we find strength, O God.
For the grace that meets us in vulnerability, we give You thanks.

G8: Lament

Thanksgiving: For this space to express our deepest laments, knowing God is intimately acquainted with our grief.
Praise Response: **In our cries, You hear us.**

Alternative:
In our lament, we find You listening and holding our sorrows, O Lord.
For the space to mourn and be heard, we offer our gratitude.

G9: HYMN AND SONG SELECTION ASSISTANT

For each Theme, the suggested hymns/songs are intended to enrich the worship experience, providing a multifaceted approach that allows for reflection, lament and the acknowledgment of God's presence in all aspects of life.

These resources aim to support congregations in respecting the solemnity of your service while facilitating a meaningful engagement with the aspects of praise and thanksgiving within these Themes. A selection of song and hymn choices for each Theme is given below.

Leaders should check the lyrics of all chosen hymns and songs to ensure they are appropriate for the context in which they will be used.

G9.1: Silence and Presence

Praise and Thanksgiving thought: Gratitude for God's silent companionship, acknowledging His presence in our solitude and silence as a source of comfort and peace.

Worship Songs/Hymns

- 'Be Still, My Soul' – This hymn encourages trust in God amid life's storms, emphasising His presence and care. (Lyricist: Catharina von Schlegel (1697–1768); trans: Jane Borthwick (1813–97); tune: *Finlandia*, composed by Jean Sibelius (1865–1957).)

- 'In Christ Alone' – Highlights the enduring presence of Christ as a cornerstone and source of strength. (Composers/Lyricists: Keith Getty (b. 1974) and Stuart Townend (b. 1963); tune: *In Christ Alone*.)

- 'Be Still and Know' by Anne (Conway) Scott (b. 1940) is a reflective piece encouraging believers to recognise God's presence in silence.

- 'Dear Refuge of My Weary Soul' – Speaks to finding solace and refuge in God's presence during times of distress. (Anne Steel (1717–1778) was the original composer; the modern adaption by Kevin Twit (b. 1964) was released in 2000.)

- 'Be Still for the Presence of the Lord' – Directly acknowledges the holy presence of God in moments of stillness. (David J. Evans (b. 1957), released in 1986.)

G9.2: Waiting (and Transformation)

Praise and Thanksgiving thought: Celebrating the transformative work that God does within us as we wait, recognising the sacredness of God's timing.

Worship Songs/Hymns

- 'Everlasting God' – Encourages waiting on the Lord for renewed strength (Brenton Brown (b. 1973)).

- 'While I'm Waiting' – A contemporary song about serving God and remaining faithful during periods of waiting (John Waller (b. 1970)).

- 'Oceans (Where Feet May Fail)' – Reflects on stepping out in faith and trusting God amid uncertainty (Hillsong Worship).

- '10,000 Reasons (Bless the Lord)' – Offers praise for God's endless blessings, recognising His work in all circumstances (Matt Redman b. (1974)).

G9.3: Darkness

Praise and Thanksgiving thought: Expressing trust and reverence for God's guidance and light, even when we walk through the darkest moments.

Worship Songs/Hymns

- **'I Will Fear No Evil'** – Reminiscent of Psalm 23, reinforcing trust in God through dark valleys. (The original is by Thais Schucman, but English translations are available.)

- **'Christ Be Our Light'** – A plea for Christ's light in a world filled with darkness and longing (Bernadette Farrell (b. 1957)).

- **'Here I Am to Worship'** – Acknowledges Christ as the light of the world coming into our darkness (Hillsong Worship).

- **'The Lord Is My Light'** – Based on Psalm 27, affirming God as our light and salvation (Nathaniel Bassey (b. 1981)).

- **'You Never Let Go'** – Matt Redman's song about God's constant presence through storms and darkness (Matt Redman (b. 1974)).

G9.4: Disorientation

Praise and Thanksgiving thought: Thankfulness for God's unchanging nature and His guidance when life feels so disorienting that the path ahead seems unclear.

Worship Songs/Hymns

- **'Lead, Kindly Light'** – An earnest prayer for guidance through the encircling gloom. (John Henry Newman (1801–1890), sung to a variety of tunes, with *Sandon* by Charles H. Purday (1799–1885) and *Alberta* by Sir William Harris (1883–1973) best suited for this context.)

- **'Guide Me, O Thou Great Jehovah'** – A hymn asking for God's guidance through the wilderness of life. (William Williams (1717–1791), and English translation by Peter Williams (1722–1796); tune: *Cwm Rhondda*, composed by John Hughes (1873–1932).)

- **'O God, Our Help in Ages Past'** – Reflects on God's eternal guidance and protection based on Psalm 90. (Isaac Watts

(1674–1748); tune: *St. Anne*, composed by William Croft (1678–1727).)

- **'Cornerstone'** – Emphasises reliance on Christ's consistent guidance and presence (Hillsong Worship).

- **'God Will Make a Way'** – A song of assurance that God provides direction even when we cannot see it (Don Moen (b. 1950)).

G9.5: Community and Witness

Praise and Thanksgiving thought: Celebrating the strength and support found in the Christian community, witnessing God's love and faithfulness through shared experiences.

Worship Songs/Hymns

- **'Blest Be the Tie That Binds'** – Highlights the spiritual connections within the community of faith. (John Fawcett (1739–1817) and sung to the tune *Dennis*, composed by Johann Georg Nägeli (1768–1836) and arranged by Lowell Mason (1792–1872).)

- **'They'll Know We Are Christians By Our Love'** – Focuses on the witness of communal Christian love (Fr. Peter Scholtes (1938–2009)).

- **'In Christ There Is No East or West'** – Celebrates unity and fellowship in Christ. (John Oxenham (1852–1941); tune: *St. Peter* by Alexander R. Reinagle (1799–1877) first published in 1836.)

- **'One Bread, One Body'** – A reminder of the unity within the Christian community despite our diversity (John B. Foley (b. 1939)).

- **'Build Your Kingdom Here'** – Encourages the Church to be a light in the darkness, seeking God's kingdom in the community (Rend Collective).

G9.6: Memory

Praise and Thanksgiving thought: Giving thanks for the gift of memory to recall God's faithfulness and love throughout our lives and history.

Worship Songs/Hymns

- 'Great Is Thy Faithfulness' – Celebrates God's unchanging faithfulness as remembered through time. (Thomas Chisholm (1866–1960) with the tune *Faithfulness*, composed by William M. Runyan (1870–1957).)

- 'Remembrance' – Commemorates Christ's sacrifice and God's love, encouraging us to remember His deeds (Hillsong Worship).

- 'Faithful One' – A song of praise to God for His unwavering presence and faithfulness (Brian Doerksen (b. 1965)).

- 'Amazing Grace' – A classic hymn that reflects on the grace and mercy of God as experienced throughout one's life. (John Newton (1725–1807); tune: *New Britain*, William Walker (1809–1875).)

G9.7: Vulnerability

Praise and Thanksgiving thought: Acknowledging our vulnerability before God as the groundwork for providing a space for grace, where we can bring our authentic selves to find acceptance and strength.

Worship Songs/Hymns

- 'Just As I Am' – An invitation to come before God with all our imperfections and vulnerabilities. (Charlotte Elliott (1789–1871); tune: *Woodworth*, William B. Bradbury (1816–1868).)

- 'Broken Vessels (Amazing Grace)' – Illustrates how God's grace and beauty are always in our lives (Joel Houston (b. 1979) and Jonas Myrin (b. 1982)).

- 'I Need Thee Every Hour' – A hymn expressing our constant need for God's presence and strength. (Annie S. Hawks (1835–1918) and Robert Lowry (1826–1899); tune: *Need*, also by Lowry.)

- 'The Power of Your Love' – Highlights the transformative power of God's love in our lives, especially in our most vulnerable moments. (Geoff Bullock (b. 1955); tune: *Lord, I Come to You* also by Bullock.)

G9.8: Lament

Praise and Thanksgiving thought: Recognising lament as a form of worship that allows us to express our deepest sorrows to God, knowing that He hears and is with us in our pain.

Worship Songs/Hymns

- 'Psalm 13' – A musical adaptation of the Psalmist's cry to God, asking how long He will seem distant, embodying the Theme of lament (Sovereign Grace Music).

- 'It Is Well With My Soul' – Even amid trials and sorrow, this hymn declares trust in God's providence. (D. S. Warner (1842–1895); tune: *Oh, blessed Jesus! Thy love is supreme* by B. E. Warren (1867–1951).)

- 'O Come, O Come, Emmanuel' – A traditional Advent hymn that captures a sense of longing and expectation, that *could be* fitting for a service in the right context. (Latin 12th Century, translated by J. M. Neale (1818–1866); tune: *Veni Emmanuel (Chant)*, anonymous composer but adapted by Thomas Helmore (1811–1890).)

H: Secular Alternatives

Several secular alternatives to hymns and explicitly Christian texts, along with a rationale for their selection, are shown below. These include poems, songs and works of art that may provide a gateway into narratives in a way that more sacred or 'church-related' materials may not.

H1: Silence and Presence

- Poem: 'Still I Rise' by Maya Angelou – while known for its themes of hope, the poem's strength also lies in its acknowledgment of the struggle, offering a powerful testament to the human spirit's resilience.

- Poem: 'The Thing Is' by Ellen Bass – this poem speaks to enduring pain and finding a way to love life again, emphasising the power of presence and acceptance amid suffering.

- Song: 'Wait it Out' by Imogen Heap – this song captures the essence of being present with ourselves regardless of our current state, acknowledging the struggle and the importance of waiting.

- Art: 'Wanderer above the Sea of Fog' by Caspar David Friedrich – emphasises the individual's contemplation and being present in the vastness of nature, reflecting on the self.

- Art: 'With My Back to the World' – minimalist works, particularly by Agnes Martin, invite contemplation and an awareness of presence through their subtle lines and colours.

H2: Waiting

- Poem: **'Patience'** by Kay Ryan – reflects on the nature of waiting as an active and profound state, focusing on the process itself rather than the outcome.

- Song: **'The Waiting'** by Tom Petty – focuses on the act of waiting as an experience in and of itself, capturing the tension and anticipation.

- Art: Andy Goldsworthy's environmental art – his temporary works, created from natural materials, emphasise the process and transient nature of life, reflecting the theme of waiting and transformation through natural processes.

H3: Darkness

- Poem: **'Aubade'** by Philip Larkin – deals with the existential dread of darkness and the inevitability of death, capturing the tension of being in a dark place.

- Song: **'Darkness on the Edge of Town'** by Bruce Springsteen – reflects on personal and communal struggles, embodying the theme of enduring through darkness.

- Song: **'Shadow'** by Birdy – captures the feeling of being overshadowed by darkness yet also hints at the presence of light, without rushing towards it.

- Art: **'The Black Paintings'** – these works by Francisco Goya, created late in his life, reflect a dark introspection and existential turmoil.

H4: Disorientation

- Poem: **'One Art'** by Elizabeth Bishop – explores loss and 'the art of losing' as an inevitable part of life, embodying the theme of disorientation in a subtle, resigned manner.

- Poem: 'Lost' by David Wagoner – based on a Native American story, it speaks directly to the theme of being lost and the guidance found in standing still and listening.

- Song: 'Lost Cause' by Beck – captures the feeling of disorientation and the acceptance of one's situation without immediate hope for reorientation.

- Art: 'Relativity' by M.C. Escher – represents a world of perpetual disorientation, challenging perceptions and encouraging viewers to accept ambiguity and complexity.

- Art: The chaotic and disorienting paintings of Francis Bacon, which vividly portray the turmoil and disorientation of human existence.

H5: Community and Witness

- Poem: 'No Man is an Island' by John Donne – emphasises the interconnectedness of all people and the importance of community and witness in the human experience.

- Song: 'People Get Ready' by The Impressions – while often interpreted through a lens of hope, the song also underscores the importance of community and collective strength in facing challenges.

- Song: 'People Help the People' by Cherry Ghost – speaks to the power of community support and the human capacity for empathy and connection.

- Art: Diego Rivera's murals – depict the struggles and strengths of communities, highlighting the importance of solidarity and collective experience.

- Art: 'The Migration Series' by Jacob Lawrence – depicts the journey and struggles of the African American migration northward, emphasising community, struggle and witness.

H6: Memory

- Poem: **'Forgetfulness'** by Billy Collins – explores the theme of memory and forgetting in a light-hearted yet poignant manner, acknowledging the complexity of memory without pushing towards hope.

- Poem: **'The Way It Is'** by William Stafford – this poem discusses the thread that runs through our lives, even when lost, holding onto the essence of memory and identity.

- Song: **'Memory Gospel'** by Moby – an instrumental that, through its haunting melody, evokes a sense of nostalgia and reflection on memories.

- Art: **'The Persistence of Memory'** by Salvador Dalí – captures the surreal nature of time and memory, inviting reflection on the fluidity and distortion of memories particularly in the context of trauma.

H7: Vulnerability

- Poem: **'An Atlas of the Difficult World'** by Adrienne Rich – speaks to the complexity of living in a troubled world, acknowledging vulnerability as an inherent part of the human condition.

- Poem: **'She Had Some Horses'** by Joy Harjo – a powerful meditation on vulnerability, identity and healing, using the metaphor of horses to explore complex emotions.

- Art: Tracey Emin's **'My Bed'** – displays the artist's own bed after a depressive episode, symbolising vulnerability and the personal spaces where we confront our deepest selves.

H8: Lament

- Poem: **'Requiem'** by Anna Akhmatova – written across decades of Soviet repression, this poem is a monumental work of mourning and memory, embodying collective and individual lament.

- Song: **'River'** by Joni Mitchell – although often considered a Christmas song, its lyrics speak to regret and longing, embodying a deep sense of lamentation and personal reflection.

- Art: Anselm Kiefer's landscapes – his works often depict desolate, post-apocalyptic scenes that confront the history and trauma of the 20th century, inviting viewers to dwell in spaces of desolation and memory without immediate redemption.

I: Ending the Service

A blessing may be used, and you may feel this is an appropriate way to end your service. These are optional short prayers of 'dismissal' that can be used to conclude services which may better suit the context.

I1: Departing in light

As we depart from this sacred pause,
may we carry with us the peace that comes from
God's unwavering presence in our moments of waiting
    and darkness.
We move forward bearing the light of hope that,
    even in silence,
God weaves our stories of disorientation into His tapestry
    of grace.

I2: Sending forth in reflection

In the stillness of our journey today,
we have dwelt in the mystery of God's silent work within us.
We now step forward, holding in our hearts the promise of
    transformation that comes from patient waiting and trust in
    God's unfailing love.

13: Prayer for courage to seek and offer help

Gracious God, as we conclude our time in Your sacred pause,
grant us the courage to seek Your presence in our lives and the
strength to offer Your love to those around us.
May we be a beacon of Your comfort and hope to all who
navigate the shadows.

14: Affirmation of God's presence in waiting and lament

As we leave, hold fast to the assurance that in every moment
of waiting,
every instance of silence, and every act of lament, God is
intimately present with us.
In our journeying and in our resting, may we find the peace that
surpasses all understanding.

15: Exploration of grace in the sacred pause

As we stand in the threshold of the sacred pause,
we embrace the fullness of this moment –
this liminal space where grace abounds in the quiet
and the unseen.
May we resist the urge to rush past this silence,
finding instead the courage to explore the depth of grace
present here and now.
We carry the richness of this pause into every breath,
every step,
recognising that in every moment of stillness,
there is a profound invitation to encounter the Divine.

Some Other Planning Considerations

Worship leaders may want to consider these ideas when planning worship:

Silence as a Worship Element

Integrate periods of silence thoughtfully throughout the service. Silence can be a powerful tool for reflection and meditation, allowing individuals to process their thoughts and emotions in a sacred space. Guide the congregation on how to use these moments for personal reflection on the Themes discussed.

Visuals and Environment

Consider the worship space's visual and environmental elements. Soft lighting; candles; or simple, unadorned spaces can help create an atmosphere conducive to reflection and solemnity.

Visuals should complement the Themes without overwhelming the senses. You may consider drawing attention to the cross if your church setting facilitates this. If using the resource for Holy Saturday services and it is your tradition to strip the altar(s) on Maundy Thursday, the bare church may offer a particularly contemplative space. However, please be aware that, for some, the cross may symbolise ongoing violence.

Personal Reflection or Testimony

If appropriate, you could include a moment for personal reflection or testimony related to the Themes. This could be a pre-recorded segment or a live sharing by someone who can speak to the experience of finding God amid waiting or darkness, ensuring it aligns with the service's contemplative nature.

Community Engagement

Encourage the congregation to engage in acts of community support and solidarity after the service. This could be in the form of prayer circles, offering resources for mental health support, or simply spaces for conversation and shared meals.

The goal is to reinforce the Theme of community and witness, showing that while we may individually journey through darkness, we do not do so alone.

Pastoral Care Accessibility

Make sure to communicate the availability of pastoral care for those who may find themselves needing support following the service. Knowing that there is someone to talk to can be a great comfort to those who might be stirred by the Themes explored.

God's Creation

Reflecting on God's creation provides a rich source of guidance and inspiration, particularly when considering the Themes that we have derived from our thinking about Holy Saturday. Nature, in its complexity and beauty, offers profound metaphors and lessons that can illuminate our understanding and spiritual practices. Here are a few aspects of creation that can serve as guides:

1 The Cycle of Seasons – just as nature cycles through seasons, our spiritual lives also experience times of growth, flourishing, decay and dormancy. Holy Saturday can be likened to the quiet of winter, where the surface seems still and lifeless, yet beneath the ground, there is preparation for new life. This teaches us the value of waiting and trusting in God's timing for remaking.

2 The Rhythms of Day and Night – the daily transition from day to night and back to day mirrors our journey through darkness back into light, reminding us that periods of darkness are natural and temporary. Holy Saturday emphasises this transition, encouraging us to find God's presence even when His light seems dim.

3 Desert and Wilderness – deserts and wilderness areas in Scripture often symbolise times of testing, disorientation and encounter with God. These landscapes remind us that spiritual desolation can be a place of deep encounter with the divine, where distractions are stripped away, and we are more acutely aware of our dependence on God.

4 Bodies of Water – water is a powerful symbol of life, purification and transformation. It can also represent chaos and the unknown. The still waters (Psalm 23) offer a metaphor for God's peace amid turmoil, while the vast, deep waters remind us of the mysteries of faith we are called to trust in, even when we cannot see the way forward.

5 Trees and Forests – trees, standing tall through seasons and storms, provide a metaphor for resilience, rootedness and growth. They remind us of the importance of being rooted in faith, drawing strength from our community (the forest), and reaching upwards towards the light, even when surrounded by darkness.

6 The Vastness of the Cosmos – the immense scale of the universe can evoke a sense of awe and smallness, reminding us of the majesty of God and our place within His creation. This perspective can be comforting during times of disorientation and vulnerability, as it reassures us of the grandeur of God's plan and presence, enveloping our individual experiences.

Copyright

Much of the wording used in this resource comes from current authorised forms of worship for the Church of England and other named sources (with permission); other parts have been created especially for the context offered.

Sample Services

We offer two very different sample services. While both have used the example of 'Holy Saturday' as a context for the liturgy, Sample Service One acknowledges that contemplation comes in the form of the cross, so it embraces a sense of suffering and vulnerability in its language. Sample Service Two recognises that such language of suffering can be problematic, so it seeks to avoid such imagery.

Approach Involving the Cross and Language of Suffering – Sample Service One

This approach recognises that the cross is central to the Christian narrative, symbolising the sacrificial love of Christ for humanity. The New Testament, particularly the Pauline epistles, frequently emphasises the cross as a fundamental aspect of Christian faith. For example, passages such as 1 Corinthians 1.18 and Galatians 6.14 highlight the significance of the cross in understanding the Christian journey. Additionally, Scripture speaks to the reality of suffering and the Christian call to share in Christ's sufferings, as reflected in Philippians 3.10. Jesus' life and ministry were marked by moments of vulnerability and suffering, offering a model for believers; prophetic references such as Isaiah 53 and direct teachings like Mark 8.34 underscore this theme.

Theologically, this approach engages with the concept of theodicy and the redemptive value found in suffering. It posits that suffering can lead to a deeper understanding and participation in the divine nature, as suggested in 1 Peter 4.13. The concept of *kenosis,* or Christ's self-emptying (Philippians 2.5–8), is central to understanding the Christian approach to suffering and vulnerability. *Kenosis* reflects Christ's willing humility and obedience, laying aside divine privilege to fully embrace human limitations. This act of self-emptying made Jesus vulnerable – open to rejection, suffering and death. However, *kenosis* itself should not be equated with suffering; rather, suffering arose as a consequence of Christ's vulnerability within a fallen world. In this way, Christ's journey invites believers to embrace vulnerability and humility as pathways to participating in His redemptive mission. It suggests that suffering, while not inherently good or desirable, can be transformed into a means of spiritual growth and deeper communion with God (1 Peter 4.13). It can encourage a faith that actively engages with the world's pain and injustice, promoting a more empathetic and action-oriented Christianity. However, it is important to note that while this approach can offer profound comfort and solidarity for those experiencing suffering and trauma – anchoring personal pain in the larger narrative of redemption – it may not be suitable for all. For some, this may be the preferred approach, but we caution against its use in trauma-informed liturgies and have provided alternative options.

Approach Avoiding Imagery of the Cross and Suffering – Sample Service Two

While fully acknowledging the significance of the cross within Christian theology, this approach deliberately avoids potentially difficult imagery, focusing instead on the biblical theme of the kingdom of God as a present reality (Luke 17.21; John 10.10). It draws attention to scriptural passages that emphasise God's love and protection as central aspects of the Christian experience, with comforting texts like Psalm 23 and Jeremiah 29.11 offering a vision of God's enduring care and hopeful future.

Theologically, this approach is grounded in an eschatological hope that looks beyond present suffering to the ultimate reconciliation and restoration of all things, as described in Revelation

21.4. It also underscores the concept of *imago Dei*, the belief that all people are created in the image of God (Genesis 1.27), which can foster a more inclusive and affirming ministry.

From a pastoral perspective, this approach can provide a safer and more welcoming space for individuals who have experienced trauma or harm associated with religious imagery or language. It can attract and nurture those who seek a positive and empowering spiritual experience, focusing on the love of God and the inherent dignity of all people. By emphasising themes of empowerment and divine love, this approach allows for a ministry that is both inclusive and sensitive to the varied experiences within a congregation.

Sample Service One

This service was designed to bring us into remembrance of the profound mystery encapsulated in the Passion, crucifixion and death of Jesus that took place yesterday. In the quiet, still ambiance of the tomb, amid the realm of the unknown, we gather to offer our worship and present our 'final tribute' to Jesus, mirroring Mary Magdalene's act of tending to His Holy Body. Just as Mary did on the original Holy Saturday, we approach today bearing the weight of sorrow, yet anchored in the hope found in God's name and love.

This service was created for those who, in times of trauma and sorrow, gaze upon the cross as a source of strength and survival. We encourage the creation of a designated area within your church for a simple cross, bereft of Christ's figure, to stand. This may be accompanied by a white cloth or a modest candle at its base, serving as a symbol of Jesus' body resting in the tomb.

AT THE TOMB OF JESUS

The Gathering

The leader says:
In the name of the Father,
and of the Son, and of the Holy Spirit.
Amen.

We come from scattered lives to meet with God.
Let us recognise His presence with us.

Silence is kept

As God's people we have gathered:
let us worship Him together.

Penitence

The leader says:
Christ Himself bore our sins in His body on the cross so that,
free from sin, we might live for righteousness;
by His wounds we have been healed.

Let us confess our sins.

Almighty God, lover of all people, giver of all grace,
look mercifully upon us who acknowledge our sins;
create in us a pure heart and a steadfast spirit;
and lead us in the paths of holiness and righteousness;
through Jesus Christ our Lord.
Amen.

The Liturgy of the Word

The reader introduces the Old Testament reading:
The first reading is taken from Lamentations 3.19–33.

The thought of my affliction and my homelessness
is wormwood and gall!
My soul continually thinks of it
and is bowed down within me.
But this I call to mind,
and therefore I have hope:

The steadfast love of the Lord never ceases,
his mercies never come to an end;
they are new every morning;
great is your faithfulness.
'The Lord is my portion,' says my soul,
'therefore I will hope in him.'

The Lord is good to those who wait for him,
to the soul that seeks him.
It is good that one should wait quietly
for the salvation of the Lord.
It is good for one to bear
the yoke in youth,
to sit alone in silence
when the Lord has imposed it,
to put one's mouth to the dust
(there may yet be hope),
to give one's cheek to the smiter,
and be filled with insults.

For the Lord will not
reject for ever.
Although he causes grief, he will have compassion
according to the abundance of his steadfast love;
for he does not willingly afflict
or grieve anyone.

At the end the reader says:
This is the word of the Lord.
Thanks be to God.

You might want to say together Psalm 22

The reader introduces the Gospel reading:
Hear the Gospel of our Lord Jesus Christ according to John.
Glory to You, O Lord.

Meanwhile, standing near the cross of Jesus were his mother, and his mother's sister, Mary the wife of Clopas, and Mary Magdalene. When Jesus saw his mother and the disciple whom he loved standing beside her, he said to his mother, 'Woman, here is your son.' Then he said to the disciple, 'Here is your mother.' And from that hour the disciple took her into his own home.

At the end the reader says:
This is the Gospel of the Lord.
Praise to You, O Christ.

The Psalm and Canticle

In this sample service, you're invited to write and say your own Psalm of Lament

After the psalm, we say together the Canticle:
Christ suffered for you, leaving you an example,
that you should follow in His steps.

He committed no sin, no guile was found on His lips,
when He was reviled, He did not revile in turn.

When He suffered, He did not threaten,
but He trusted Himself to God who judges justly.

Christ Himself bore our sins in His body on the tree,
that we might die to sin and live to righteousness.

By His wounds, you have been healed,
for you were straying like a sheep,
but have now returned
to the shepherd and guardian of your soul.

Glory to the Father,
and to the Son,
and to the Holy Spirit.
As it was in the beginning,
is now, and ever shall be:
world without end.
Amen.

The Creed

The leader says:
We say together the Creed:

I believe in the Father, who hears our cries,
in Jesus Christ, who lamented over Jerusalem and cried out in
forsakenness,
and in the Holy Spirit, who intercedes for us with groans too
deep for words.
In my lament, I am joined to the suffering of Christ, finding in
my cries a sacred echo of His own,
a lament that is held and honoured by the Trinity, assuring me
that in my deepest pain,
I am not alone, but deeply connected to the heart of God.
Amen.

The Prayers

The intercessor introduces prayers:
We bring our sorrows, our struggles, our doubts into the
presence of God and of each other
on the day when the whole creation pauses to mourn the death
of the Saviour of the world.

Over the dignity of creation that has been neglected, used, hurt
and side-lined,
We lament.

Over the peace lost, restoration that is not yet present, and
reconciliation that is still far away,
We lament.

Over human indifference, greed, and a deep sense of injustice,
We lament.

Over human promises not being fulfilled, trust broken, hope
abandoned,
We lament.

Over those who have been hurt, silenced, not believed,
We lament.

Over those who have been powerless and trapped in their circumstances,
We lament.

Over those who have been wounded by the society and by the Church,
We lament.

Over those who have lost faith and lost hope,
We lament.

We bring our sorrows, our struggles, our doubts into the presence of God and of each other
on the day when the whole creation pauses to mourn the death of the Saviour of the world.

**Merciful Father, accept our lamentations,
for the sake of Your Son, our Saviour, Jesus Christ.
Amen.**

Alternatively, you might prefer using your own prayers or the Stations of the Cross (focused on the cross), as offered in this resource booklet, instead of the prayers suggested here.

The Lord's Prayer

The leader begins the Lord's Prayer:
As we stand at the tomb, after the events of the cross, let us pray as our Saviour has taught us:

**Our Father, who art in heaven,
hallowed be Thy name;
Thy kingdom come;
Thy will be done;
on earth as it is in heaven.
Give us this day our daily bread.
And forgive us our trespasses,**

as we forgive those who trespass against us.
And lead us not into temptation;
but deliver us from evil.
For Thine is the kingdom,
the power and the glory
for ever and ever.
Amen.

The Praise and Thanksgiving

The leader announces the hymn:
We sing together 'Were you there'

Were you there when they crucified my Lord?
Were you there when they crucified my Lord?
(Oh, sometimes it causes me to tremble, tremble, tremble)
Were you there when they crucified my Lord?

Were you there when they nailed him to the cross?
Were you there when they nailed him to the cross?
(Oh, sometimes it causes me to tremble, tremble, tremble)
Were you there when they nailed him to the cross?

Were you there when they laid him in the tomb?
Were you there when they laid him in the tomb?
(Oh, sometimes it causes me to tremble, tremble, tremble)
Were you there when they laid him in the tomb?

Were you there when the stone was rolled away?
Were you there when the stone was rolled away?
(Oh, sometimes it causes me to tremble, tremble, tremble)
Were you there when the stone was rolled away?

The Conclusion

Gracious God,
as we conclude our time in Your sacred pause,
grant us the courage to seek Your presence in our lives
and the strength to offer Your love to those around us.
May we be a beacon of Your comfort and hope to all who
navigate the shadows.
Amen.

Sample Service Two

This service aims to hold the grief of Good Friday, while also dwelling in the seemingly hopeless reality of Holy Saturday. It intentionally draws attention away from the cross and violence of Good Friday. It is envisioned that this service will be held in a church that has already stripped its altar on Maundy Thursday, and you are asked to consider that any visible crosses or crucifixes may be, for some, a symbol of ongoing violence.

A SERVICE EXPLORING THE SILENCE, WAITING AND PRESENCE OF HOLY SATURDAY

The Gathering

We come from scattered lives to meet with God.
Let us recognise His presence with us.

Silence is kept

As God's people we have gathered:
let us worship Him together.

The Introduction

The leader may introduce the service. This is an opportunity to signpost where pastoral care support can be sought during or after the service.

The leader invites the people to confession

Prayers of Penitence

Beloved community, as we abide in the solemnity of Holy
Saturday, we may find ourselves in a place of profound
uncertainty and reflection, reminiscent of the disciples' vigil.
We are invited to pause and dwell in this liminal space, where
light has not yet pierced the shadow. Let us confess our sins
as an act of trust in the God who walks with us through
every darkness, every moment of waiting, and every season of
disorientation.

Pause for reflection

O God, who is ever-present in the midst of our deepest night,
we come before You in the stillness of this day, hearts heavy
and spirits sombre,
reflecting on the disciples' own bewilderment and sorrow on
that first Holy Saturday.

Pause for reflection

**We confess, O Lord, that like them, we too find ourselves
disoriented by life's trials,
daunted by the shadows that linger and perplexed by the
silences where we expected Your voice.**

**We admit our struggles, our quickness to despair,
and our slowness to remember Your steadfast presence in all
things.**

Pause for reflection

**In Your boundless mercy, meet us here in the depths of our
vulnerability.
Forgive us for our doubts, our fears and the ways we fail to
trust in Your abiding love.**

**Grant us the grace to endure this in-between, to find solace in
the mystery,
and to hold space for our grief and confusion, knowing that
You, O God, are with us in our waiting.**

Give us the strength to embrace the discomfort of not knowing, and to find peace in the promise that You are God, even in the silence, even in the darkness.

Help us to bear witness to each other's journeys, to offer love where there is pain, and to extend grace where there is faltering.

In this sacred pause, renew our spirits and bind us together in the fellowship of shared uncertainty, that we may support one another.

Amen.

Liturgy of the Word

Ecclesiastes 3.1–8

> For everything there is a season, and a time for every matter under heaven: a time to be born, and a time to die;
> a time to plant, and a time to pluck up what is planted;
> a time to kill, and a time to heal;
> a time to break down, and a time to build up;
> a time to weep, and a time to laugh;
> a time to mourn, and a time to dance;
> a time to throw away stones, and a time to gather stones together;
> a time to embrace, and a time to refrain from embracing;
> a time to seek, and a time to lose;
> a time to keep, and a time to throw away;
> a time to tear, and a time to sew;
> a time to keep silence, and a time to speak; a time to love, and a time to hate;
> a time for war, and a time for peace.

Luke 23.6–9

> When Pilate heard this, he asked whether the man was a Galilean. And when he learned that he was under Herod's jurisdiction, he sent him off to Herod, who was himself in

Jerusalem at that time. When Herod saw Jesus, he was very glad, for he had been wanting to see him for a long time, because he had heard about him and was hoping to see him perform some sign. He questioned him at some length, but Jesus gave him no answer.

Responding to the Word

Musicians: 'The Lord is My Light'

The musicians will sing 'The Lord is My Light', which is a hymn based on Psalm 27. Continue to hold an atmosphere of waiting as we dwell in the darkness of Holy Saturday. Remind people gathered that as we wait, we trust that God holds us in this space. In the darkness of Holy Saturday, we seek God's guidance and draw upon the promise that darkness is as light to Him.

The opportunity to light a votive candle
The leader invites people to respond to this promise, if they choose/would like to, by coming forward to the bare altar to light a candle

A Period of Silence

A period of silence is held

The leader could remind people where pastoral support is located if needed during this time

A Poem

Insert a poem, for example 'Lost' by David Wagoner

A pause for silence

Affirmation of Faith

The leader invites people to stand, if comfortable to do so, to affirm our faith together

I believe in the Father, who shaped the silence of the universe,
in the Son, who walked quietly among us,
and in the Spirit, who whispers truth in moments of solitude.
This divine silence surrounds me, affirming God's presence in the quiet.

Prayers

The leader invites people to find a position that is comfortable for them in prayer

Almighty God, we find ourselves in a sacred pause,
we hold space for our grief, our uncertainties, and the deep yearnings of our hearts.
Grant us, O Lord, the grace to dwell here with faith and patience.
Teach us to listen for Your still, small voice in the midst of our waiting,
reminding us that even in the darkest night,
Your love and presence are unwavering.

Comfort all who carry the weight of trauma and loss,
enveloping them in Your peace that surpasses understanding.
Strengthen our community, that we offer solace and support on journeys through the shadows.

As we reflect on the mystery of Your love, help us to feel Your grace.
May this time draw us closer to You and to each other,
forging bonds of compassion and understanding.

We ask this in the name of Jesus Christ, as we wait in the silence of the tomb.
Amen.

The Lord's Prayer

Lord, remember us in Your kingdom
as we pray in the words You gave us.
Our Father, who art in heaven,
hallowed be Thy name;
Thy kingdom come;
Thy will be done;
on earth as it is in heaven.
Give us this day our daily bread.
And forgive us our trespasses,
as we forgive those who trespass against us.
And lead us not into temptation;
but deliver us from evil.
For Thine is the kingdom,
the power and the glory
for ever and ever.
Amen.

Hymn

Hymn: 'Be Still and Know'

*The words of the hymn are below. Remind people to feel free to
join in or listen and reflect as appropriate.*

Be still and know that I am God x4
I am the Lord that leadeth thee x4
In Thee, O Lord, I put my trust x4

Conclusion

Encourage people to leave the space in silence. Remind everyone that the pastoral care team are at hand after the service if it should be helpful to talk or pray with someone else.

The leader says the final prayer:
As we depart from this sacred pause, may we carry with us the peace that comes from God's unwavering presence in our moments of waiting and darkness.
We go forth, bearing the light of hope that, even in silence God weaves our stories of disorientation into His tapestry of grace.
Amen.

Prayers Inspired by the Authors

Prayer inspired by Stephanie Foo
(*What My Bones Know*)

Gracious God, in the midst of pain, there is a space for grace
without the immediate rush to hope. In our journey through
the wilderness of our souls, help us to hold onto that grace,
acknowledging our pain without being consumed by it. Guide
us in the complex journey of healing as we navigate the return
of memories or the appearance of triggers, fighting each battle
with Your strength anew. May we find solace in Your presence,
the unchanging constant in our ever-changing struggle. Amen.

Prayer inspired by Jennifer Baldwin
(*Trauma-Sensitive Theology*)

Healing Spirit, speak to the restoration of divine energy
through life and relationships as the source of true salvation.
As we navigate our lives, we ask for Your soothing presence to
heal and unburden the wounds and beliefs that may have been
inflicted upon us. May our communities find unity in Your
compassionate wisdom, and may individuals feel reconnected
to the loving awareness of their whole selves, reducing the felt
separation from You and the global web of life. Amen.

Intercession inspired by Edith Eger
(*The Choice*)

Lord of Liberation, teach us the power of choice in the aftermath of trauma – the choice to dismantle the prisons of our mind, brick by brick. Today we pray for the strength to accept what is, to forgive ourselves, and to open our hearts to the miracles that exist now. In the sacred present, help us to reclaim our inner truth, our strength and our innocence. May we live now with the freedom of accepting Your grace, finding peace in the acceptance of our reality. Amen.

Collect inspired by Selina Stone
(*Tarry Awhile*)

Eternal Companion, illuminate the essential role of darkness in the journey of creation and life itself. In the quiet and absence of light (this Holy Saturday), remind us that darkness is not devoid of Your Spirit but is rather the prime space for Your work within us. Transform us as we sit in silent prayer, overturning the harmful silences that have held us captive. In this day of darkness, may we find the courage to embrace the fertile ground from which new life springs. Come, Lord Jesus, and make Your hidden work in us known. Amen.

In The Sacred Pause

While we anticipate the dawn of Easter, we have striven to hold the sacred space of Holy Saturday in our hearts, drawing upon the grace found in its contemplation to shape our spiritual journey throughout the entire liturgical year. Grounded in the assurance of God's unfailing presence with us, every day and every step of the way, these reflections extend beyond a single day, offering guidance and comfort in all seasons of life.

We are not saying that there is no hope or that Hell is hopelessness. We are saying that there is hope in being in this present space, place and time. That there is grace and love to be found in the now as there was on Holy Saturday.

If that hope is hopelessness refusing to give up, or a recognition that carrying the cross to justice can plant seeds of love, then that may be hope enough.

Appendix

Prayers of Absolution

Due to theological, pastoral and canonical considerations, it has not been possible to include Prayers of Absolution in the liturgies in *In the Sacred Pause*. The reasons are as follows.

First, within the Church of England, clergy are restricted – within formal public liturgical settings – from composing or using alternative forms of absolution beyond those already authorised. *In the Sacred Pause* offers newly crafted, trauma-informed liturgies, and the inclusion of an unauthorised absolution could have conflicted with these canonical requirements. We note that Canon B5(4) provides for authorised variations, and that an absolution-type prayer may be offered where a priest is present.

Second, the book was designed to support laity-led services, particularly in settings where ordained leadership might not be present or appropriate. Absolution, by its sacramental nature, is traditionally reserved for priestly ministry. To ensure accessibility and avoid creating an imbalance in leadership, the decision was made to exclude both absolution and priestly blessings.

Finally, and perhaps most significantly, trauma theology informed this choice. In contexts of deep wounding, the language of absolution – while profoundly meaningful – can sometimes feel misapplied, especially where religious frameworks have historically been used to reinforce guilt or shame. Instead, these liturgies seek to assure participants of God's grace and presence, and of the Church's ongoing work of remaking, without imposing a structure that might inadvertently trigger difficult associations.

The omission does not diminish the power of forgiveness, but reflects an understanding that remaking is often an iterative journey rather than a moment of immediate resolution. Where a priest is present and wishes to include an absolution, they are encouraged to use an authorised text appropriate to their context.

Ultimately, *In the Sacred Pause* seeks to hold space for worship that is inclusive, sensitive and attuned to the complexities of lived experience, trusting that God's mercy flows abundantly within and beyond formal declarations.

References and Further Reading

Scripture quotations are from New Revised Standard Version Bible: Anglicised Edition.

Adam, David, 2008, *The Rhythm of Life: Celtic Daily Prayer*, London: SPCK.

Bond, Lucy and Stef Craps, 2020, *Trauma*, London and New York: Routledge.

Celebrating Common Prayer: The Daily Office SSF, 1992, Joint Advisory Panel, Bristol: Mowbray.

Colquhoun, Frank, 2005, *New Parish Prayers*, new edn, London: Hodder & Stoughton.

Common Worship: Daily Prayer, 2013, The Archbishops' Council of the Church of England.

Common Worship: Times and Seasons, 2013, The Archbishops' Council of the Church of England.

Jones, Serene, 2009, *Trauma and Grace: Theology in a Ruptured World*, Louisville, KY: Westminster John Knox Press.

Kolk, Bessel van der, 2015, *The Body Keeps the Score: Mind, Brain and Body in the Transformation of Trauma*, London: Penguin.

O'Donnell, Karen, 2018, *Broken Bodies: The Eucharist, Mary and the Body in Trauma Theology*, London: SCM Press.

O'Donnell, Karen, 2022, *The Dark Womb: Re-Conceiving Theology through Reproductive Loss*. London: SCM Press.

New Patterns of Worship, 2019, The Archbishop's Council, London: Church House Publishing.

Rambo, Shelly, 2010, *Spirit and Trauma: A Theology of Remaining*, Louisville, Kentucky: Westminster John Knox Press.

Riley, Cole Arthur, 2024, *Black Liturgies*, Toronto: Penguin Random House.

Acknowledgements of Copyright Sources

The authors and publisher are grateful for permission to reproduce material under copyright and in particular to:

The Rhythm of Life – Celtic Daily Prayer by David Adam. © SPCK Publishing. Used with permission.

New Parish Prayers (New Edition) by Frank Colquhoun. © Hodder Faith. Used with acknowledgment.

Celebrating Common Prayer – the Daily Office SSF. © Society of St. Francis, 27th Nov 2003. Used by permission of Bloomsbury Publishing Plc.

Common Worship and *New Patterns for Worship*. © The Archbishops' Council. Used with permission.